STAR WARS™

BOOK OF LISTS

BY COLE HORTON

TITAN BOOKS

To Jennifer and Juliana

INTRODUCTION

When creator and director George Lucas first envisioned the story of *Star Wars*, the space opera he wanted to make was too large for any one film. He imagined a story so big it would take an unheard-of nine films to tell. He would have to settle for just one, a film then known only as *Star Wars* (now, *A New Hope*). That film told the middle story of an epic battle between the forces of good and evil, and surprised almost everyone to become one of the most successful films of all time. Now more than forty years and 11 films later, *Star Wars* has grown even larger than anyone could have imagined.

The subsequent films, *The Empire Strikes Back* (1980) and *Return of the Jedi* (1983), took us to new places, gave us more villains to root against, and showed us a hopeful vision of a galaxy far, far away. We saw the fall of an Empire, the redemption of Darth Vader and rise of Luke Skywalker as a Jedi Knight, cementing these characters into the hearts and minds of a generation.

In 1999, more than twenty years after the first *Star Wars*, audiences got to see first-hand galactic events only alluded to in earlier installments. These prequel films—*The Phantom Menace* (1999), *Attack of the Clones* (2002), and *Revenge of the Sith* (2005) showed us the fall of Anakin Sky-walker, revealed the shocking rise of Darth Vader, took us to the battlefields of the Clone Wars, and portrayed what the Jedi Order had been.

The story of the Jedi came back to the big screen in a new trilogy, beginning with *The Force Awakens* (2015). There, a fresh generation of protagonists join the classic heroes in a renewed struggle against the dark side. In *The Last Jedi* (2017), we learn what happened to Jedi Master Luke Skywalker and in *The Rise of Skywalker* (2019), we see the epic conclusion of the Sky-walker saga.

But the Skywalker story is just one part of a galaxy far, far way. Films like *Rogue One: A Star Wars Story* (2016) and *Solo: A Star Wars Story* (2018) give us new insights into the events and characters we'd come to know and love. Whether it's the rebel mission to steal the Death Star plans or the story behind Han Solo's scoundrel ways, they added even more epic scale to the *Star Wars* galaxy.

That epic scale is part of what makes *Star Wars* so great. Audiences are thrust into the middle of the action, diving head first into a galaxy of unending possibilities. It's a story that spills onto the pages of hundreds of books and comics, comes home in animated and live-action series, rests in our hands in dozens of games, and fills our imagination thanks to countless toys. That epic scale is on display in these 100 lists as well. They reveal many of the recurring themes, common elements, and familiar motifs from the films that make *Star Wars* an enduring story for generations of fans.

CONTENTS

CHAPTER 1:
MAJOR FIGURES OF THE GALAXY

"I AM A JEDI, LIKE MY FATHER BEFORE ME"

LUKE SKYWALKER'S MOST HEROIC MOMENTS

A BACKWATER FARM BOY DOESN'T BECOME THE MOST LEGENDARY HERO IN GALACTIC HISTORY WITHOUT HIS FAIR SHARE OF COURAGEOUS ACTS. WHEN LUKE SKYWALKER EMBARKS ON THE ULTIMATE HERO'S JOURNEY, LITTLE DOES HE KNOW THAT SO MANY DARING MOMENTS LIE AHEAD OF HIM. BEFORE HE'S DONE, HE'LL TAKE DOWN A DEATH STAR, DEFEAT AN EMPEROR, AND BECOME LEGENDARY ACROSS THE GALAXY.

DEATH STAR ESCAPE
(*A New Hope*)

During the rescue of Princess Leia on the planet-destroying Death Star battle station, Luke and the princess face a perilous challenge. With stormtroopers not far behind and a broken bridge ahead of them, Luke uses a grappling hook to swing across a seemingly endless chasm below. With a skilled toss of the rope and a kiss for luck, Luke carries Leia safely across the abyss to their eventual escape. (**Image A**)

DEATH STAR TRENCH RUN
(*A New Hope*)

Just moments after becoming a rebel, Luke joins two squadrons of brave starfighter pilots in their last-ditch effort to destroy the Death Star. Their plan is to fly the tiny fighters through the station's defenses and target a weakness in the superweapon's design. With the fate of the Rebellion resting on his aim and Darth Vader on his tail, Luke uses the Force to make a one-in-a-million shot that destroys the battle station and saves the galaxy. (Image B)

BATTLE OF HOTH
(*The Empire Strikes Back*)

Now the leader of Rogue Squadron, Commander Luke Skywalker leads a gallant defense of the rebel base on Hoth. As Imperial walkers—unfazed by laser blasts—bear down upon the fleeing rebels, Luke and his pilots employ cables to trip the mechanical monsters. When his own speeder goes down, Luke uses his lightsaber (and a few gadgets) to take down a walker single-handedly.

RESCUE ON TATOOINE
(*Return of the Jedi*)

When the vile gangster Jabba the Hutt finally captures Han Solo, Luke stages a heroic rescue attempt of his friend. Just when it looks like the whole gang will be executed, Luke puts his plan into motion. With some help from R2-D2, the Jedi saves his friends, destroys Jabba's sail barge. It's all in a day's work for the growing Jedi. (**Image C**)

DUEL WITH VADER
(*Return of the Jedi*)

Luke faces his father, Darth Vader, and the evil Galactic Emperor in this climactic lightsaber duel aboard the second Death Star. Sensing good in him, Luke hopes to turn his father back to the light side but the Emperor has other plans. Courageously, the young Skywalker proclaims he will not fight anymore, tossing his lightsaber to the side. As the Emperor hands out a shocking punishment to the young man, Vader does indeed have a change of heart and sacrifices himself to defeat the Emperor. (**Image D**)

BATTLE OF CRAIT
(*The Last Jedi*)

Decades after defeating the Empire, Luke Skywalker goes into hiding on the distant planet of Ahch-To. The aging Jedi Master's self-exile comes after his failure to train the next generation of Jedi and his nephew Ben Solo's turn to the dark side. A visit from Rey, R2-D2, and Chewbacca isn't enough to convince him to return to civilization, but the wisdom of his long-lost Master Yoda persuades Luke that he must step in to save the Resistance from the evil First Order. Luke projects himself to the planet of Crait with the power of the Force where he confronts Kylo Ren. While the effort tricks his former student and allows the Resistance to escape, it is also fatally exhausting to Skywalker. As a result of his heroic deed, Luke Skywalker becomes one with Force. (**Image E**)

RECALCITRANT ROYAL

LEIA ORGANA'S MOST DEFIANT MOMENTS

PRINCESS LEIA ORGANA IS NO DAMSEL IN DISTRESS. ACROSS THE *STAR WARS* SAGA, SHE'S STOOD UP TO SOME OF THE BIGGEST BADDIES THE GALAXY HAS TO OFFER. WHETHER ACTING AS A SENATOR, ROYAL, REBEL, OR GENERAL, LEIA'S DEFIANCE SEEMINGLY DEFINES THIS LEADER WHO WEARS MANY HATS. THESE ARE THE TIMES WHERE LEIA STOOD STRONG IN THE FACE OF DANGER.

A

DARTH VADER
(*A New Hope*)

While fleeing with the stolen Death Star schematic, Leia is captured by Darth Vader who demands to know what she has done with the plans. Having just handed the plans to R2-D2 moments before, she calmly stands toe-to-toe with a Sith Lord and tells him, "I don't know what you're talking about." Vader then takes her captive on the Death Star and uses a mind probe to get her to talk but she doesn't break under pressure. (**Image A**)

GRAND MOFF TARKIN
(*A New Hope*)

Aboard the Death Star, Leia doesn't back down from Grand Moff Tarkin, one of the leading figures in the Empire. She casually says, "Governor Tarkin, I should have expected to find you holding Vader's leash. I recognized your foul stench when I was brought on board." That's two insults in as many sentences.

ECHO BASE
(*The Empire Strikes Back*)

After years of hiding, the Empire finally discovers the Rebellion's hidden base on the planet Hoth. Rebel leaders order a full evacuation as Imperial ground troops inch closer. As top leadership escapes, Leia stays until nearly the very end. She gets out aboard the *Millennium Falcon* just moments before Darth Vader arrives. (**Image B**)

JABBA THE HUTT
(*Return of the Jedi*)

When her rescue attempt of Han Solo goes awry, Leia becomes the prisoner of Jabba the Hutt. The disgusting gangster keeps her close at hand, chained by the neck to his dais. It's a disgraceful position for a royal, but it does not last long. Leia turns that chain into a weapon, chokes the Hutt to death, and escapes to fight another day.

THE FIRST ORDER
(*The Force Awakens*)

Leia Organa, having served during peacetime in the Senate, returns to her warrior roots leading up to the events of *The Force Awakens*. Now a general, she is one of the few leaders in the galaxy to realize the danger posed by the First Order. After the First Order destroys the New Republic using their Starkiller Base superweapon, Leia and her band of Resistance fighters are the last ones left to stand up to their enemy's might. Once again, Leia finds herself in a familiar, defiant position. (**Image C**)

"HEY, IT'S ME!"

SOLO'S BEST ONE-LINERS

HAN SOLO IS MANY THINGS: SMUGGLER, PILOT, REBEL, FATHER, AND FRIEND. BUT NO MATTER WHAT ROLE HE PLAYS, HAN ALWAYS HAS A WAY WITH WORDS. BUT THE QUESTION REMAINS, DO THESE ONE-LINERS GET HAN INTO MORE TROUBLE THAN THEY GET HIM OUT OF?

"I'VE GOT A REALLY GOOD FEELING ABOUT THIS."
(*Solo: A Star Wars Story*)

Before he was a hardened smuggler, young Han Solo was more of an optimist. Without such a positive attitude, he wouldn't have been crazy enough to make the Kessel Run. (**Image A**)

"WHEN HAVE I EVER STEERED YOU WRONG?"
(*Solo: A Star Wars Story*)

Foreshadowing the next four decades of misadventures, Han assures his new friend Chewbacca that everything will be alright. It certainly won't be.

"IT'S THE SHIP THAT MADE THE KESSEL RUN IN LESS THAN TWELVE PARSECS."
(*A New Hope*)

Han's most notable achievement is even true, if you round down.

"HOKEY RELIGIONS AND ANCIENT WEAPONS ARE NO MATCH FOR A GOOD BLASTER AT YOUR SIDE."
(*A New Hope*)

Han will eventually have a change of heart when it comes to the Force, but in his younger years he isn't shy about his opinion of the Jedi.

"YOU KNOW, SOMETIMES I AMAZE EVEN MYSELF."
(*A New Hope*)

Proud of his escape from the Death Star, Han isn't afraid to brag at his accomplishment. Little does he know they are being tracked.

"GREAT KID! DON'T GET COCKY."
(*A New Hope*)

Luke Skywalker might have destroyed his first TIE fighter, but the experienced smuggler knows that the fight isn't over yet. (**Image B**)

"LAUGH IT UP, FUZZBALL."
(*The Empire Strikes Back*)

Han doesn't find Leia's insults quite as funny as Chewbacca does.

"I KNOW."
(*The Empire Strikes Back*)

When Leia professes, "I love you," Han's response is fit for a scoundrel.

"FLY CASUAL."
(*Return of the Jedi*)

As they fly a stolen shuttle into enemy territory, it's hard to tell if Han is trying to reassure his crew—or himself—that everything will be alright.

"HEY, IT'S ME."
(*Return of the Jedi*)

Han being Han is exactly what everyone else is worried about.

"CHEWIE, WE'RE HOME."
(*The Force Awakens*)

After years apart from their beloved *Millennium Falcon*, Han need not say any more to convey the sense of relief when they finally step onboard once again. (**Image C**)

"THAT'S NOT HOW THE FORCE WORKS!"
(*The Force Awakens*)

Finn's plan to infiltrate Starkiller Base isn't much of a plan at all. He just assumes they can "use the Force" and figure it out along the way, but even Han Solo knows that isn't how the Force works. (**Image D**)

IT'S NOT WISE TO UPSET A WOOKIEE

CHEWBACCA'S BEST TEMPER TANTRUMS

CHEWBACCA MIGHT SEEM LIKE A GENTLE GIANT, BUT THIS OVER 200-YEAR-OLD WOOKIEE HAS SOUNDLY EARNED THE REPUTATION FOR BEING MIGHTY. HIS TEMPER CAN SOMETIMES GET THE BEST OF HIM, ESPECIALLY IN STRESSFUL SITUATIONS. STEER CLEAR WHEN THIS WALKING CARPET GETS UPSET!

"THE BEAST" OF MIMBAN
(*Solo: A Star Wars Story*)

Han Solo first meets Chewbacca under the worst of circumstances. The Empire punishes deserters by throwing them in a pit with the starving, captive Wookiee. Chewbacca might have been the end of Han Solo, had the smooth-talking scoundrel not convinced him to direct his anger at the Imperials. The duo escapes together and they form a life-long friendship.

HOLOCHESS
(*Solo: A Star Wars Story*, *A New Hope*)

Chewbacca enjoys a good game of holochess aboard the *Millennium Falcon*, but only if he's winning. Tobias Beckett tries to teach Chewie how to play, but the Wookiee just takes his anger out at the table. Years later, C-3PO and R2-D2 are warned that it's just best to let the Wookiee win.

KESSEL
(*Solo: A Star Wars Story*)

On a heist mission to steal raw hyperfuel from the spice mines of Kessel, Chewbacca encounters fellow Wookiees that have been enslaved by the Pyke Syndicate. Enraged at what he finds, Chewie breaks with the plan to free his people, teaching the guards a thing or two about legendary Wookiee anger in the process!

FIXING THE *FALCON*
(*The Empire Strikes Back*)

Han and Chewie's struggles to maintain their ship, the *Millennium Falcon*, prove to be an ongoing challenge for the team. As Chewbacca tries to get the ship repaired so the duo can leave the planet Hoth, sparks fly, alarms sound, and Chewbacca's angry snarls ring out through the hangar at Echo Base.

CLOUD CITY CARBON-FREEZING CHAMBER
(*The Empire Strikes Back*)

Han Solo's betrayal and capture at Cloud City rightfully angers Chewbacca. The defiant Wookiee begins tossing stormtroopers to the side before Han calms his old friend. Chewie must wait to fight another day.

CHOKING LANDO CALRISSIAN
(*The Empire Strikes Back*)

Betraying Han Solo brings the full wrath of Chewbacca down on Lando Calrissian. Luckily, the scoundrel has a plan to save Solo, if only he can get the words out while being choked at the hands of Chewbacca.

FINN'S FIRST AID
(*The Force Awakens*)

When Chewbacca is wounded at the Battle of Takodana, Finn is the unlucky one who must apply first aid to the ailing Wookiee. Chewbacca doesn't take the pain gracefully.

PORG COPILOTS
(*The Last Jedi*)

Chewbacca didn't ask for a porg infestation on the *Falcon*, but that's just what he gets after a trip to Ahch-To. The curious little birds make his ship their home, nesting in the hallways, biting at the upholstery, and interfering with Chewie as he pilots the ship at the Battle of Crait. They're too cute to do anything about, so Chewie can only voice his anger.

MAY THE FORCE BE WITH YOU

UNIQUE AND USEFUL WAYS THE FORCE HAS BEEN USED

THE FORCE IS MUCH MORE THAN A RELIGION; IT'S A DOWNRIGHT USEFUL TOOL. WHILE IT FLOWS THROUGH EVERY LIVING THING, NOT EVERYONE CAN TAP INTO ITS POWER. THIS RARE GIFT ALLOWS THOSE WHO CAN CONTROL IT TO EXHIBIT SOME EXCEPTIONAL ABILITIES. THESE ARE SOME OF THE UNIQUE AND USEFUL WAYS TO USE THE FORCE.

PILOTING A PODRACER
(*The Phantom Menace*)

Podracing is a fast, dangerous, and often illegal sport. The two giant engines strapped to a tiny cockpit go so fast that humans can't even pilot them. That is, unless you have the heightened senses of a Jedi. Anakin Skywalker is the only human to pilot a podracer thanks to his Force abilities, which allow him to compete with the greatest racers the galaxy has to offer. (**Image A**)

CHEATING FOR A GOOD CAUSE
(*The Phantom Menace*)

Does it count as cheating if you do it to save the galaxy? That's exactly what Jedi Master Qui-Gon Jinn thought he was doing by making a bet with the gambling junk dealer Watto. On the line: young Anakin Skywalker's freedom. They rolled the dice, and thanks to a little push from the Force, the odds were in the Jedi's favor.

MIND TRICKS
(*A New Hope*)

Luke Skywalker can't believe his eyes when Obi-Wan Kenobi tricks Imperial stormtroopers into letting them through a security checkpoint. Little does he know that those weak-minded stormtroopers didn't stand a chance against the Jedi Master's exceedingly convincing mind tricks. (**Image B**)

THE LIGHTSABER REACH
(*The Empire Strikes Back*)

Being ambushed by a deadly snow creature and hung up as an afternoon snack might be a problem for most people, but Luke Skywalker isn't most people. The Jedi-in-training channels all of his concentration to snatch his lightsaber from a nearby snowdrift, cut himself free, and lop off the arm of the wampa monster keeping him there. (**Image C**)

LEVITATE A DEITY
(*Return of the Jedi*)

Ewoks are small, furry, and strangely religious. When they mistake C-3PO for a god, Luke Skywalker seizes on the misunderstanding to get himself out of captivity. At first, the Ewoks refuse C-3PO's request to set his friends free, but after Luke lifts the droid high into the air with the Force, the Ewoks think twice about questioning an order. (**Image D**)

EXCAVATION
(*The Last Jedi*)

With the First Order closing in, members of the Resistance find their escape route on Crait to be blocked by a mountain of rubble. Their rebellion would have been finished if not for Rey's arrival on the other side. She reaches out with the Force, lifts every stone out of their path, and gives the survivors the chance to fight another day.

EXCEPTIONAL ACROBATICS
(*The Rise of Skywalker*)

Never mind timing it right, the ability to do a backflip over a TIE fighter as it tries to run you over is an impossible feat. That is, unless you are Rey. She's got the speed, stamina, and Force-filled reflexes to take the leap and nail the landing, once again getting the best of Kylo Ren. (**Image E**)

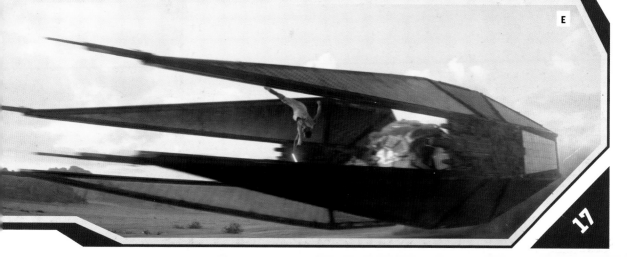

A CERTAIN POINT OF VIEW

SOME OF THE MOST ENIGMATIC JEDI QUOTES

THE ONLY THING MORE MYSTERIOUS THAN THE FORCE MIGHT BE THE WISDOM OF THE JEDI WHO FOLLOW IT. JEDI MASTERS AREN'T ALWAYS THE MOST STRAIGHTFORWARD BEINGS, AS THESE ENIGMATIC QUOTES ILLUSTRATE. TRY TO KEEP UP. YOU MIGHT JUST LEARN SOMETHING.

"HE IS THE CHOSEN ONE . . . YOU MUST SEE IT." -QUI-GON JINN
(*The Phantom Menace*)

The prophecy of the Chosen One who will bring balance to the Force is not initially explained. While the Jedi Council all seem up to speed and Qui-Gon makes a convincing case that young Anakin Skywalker is the Chosen One, the audience is left to wonder what it all means.

"YOUR FATHER WANTED YOU TO HAVE THIS WHEN YOU WERE OLD ENOUGH." -OBI-WAN KENOBI
(*A New Hope*)

As he hands Luke Skywalker his father's old lightsaber, Obi-Wan isn't exactly telling the truth about how he came to own the weapon. After all, Kenobi left Luke's father for dead beside a river of lava, pocketing the old saber as he walked away. Nearly two decades later, the old master's retelling paints a rosier picture of history about Anakin's intentions.

"ONLY WHAT YOU TAKE WITH YOU." -YODA
(*The Empire Strikes Back*)

When Yoda sends Luke Skywalker into a mysterious cave, he doesn't exactly give the young Jedi much info about what lies ahead. Luke has no idea that he will come face to face with a vision of Darth Vader.

"NO, THERE IS ANOTHER." -YODA
(*The Empire Strikes Back*)

When Obi-Wan Kenobi comments that Luke Skywalker is their last hope to save the galaxy, Yoda reminds them there is another. Audiences had no idea at the time that they were referring to Luke's sister, Leia. Why would they? Just moments before the two had kissed!

**"WE ARE WHAT THEY GROW BEYOND."
-YODA**
(*The Last Jedi*)

Now a master himself, Luke continues to benefit from Yoda's experience as a teacher. Both share in the joys and frustrations of passing on what they know to the next generation of Jedi.

**"NO ONE'S EVER REALLY GONE."
-LUKE SKYWALKER**
(*The Last Jedi*)

Before his selfless sacrifice to save the Resistance at Crait, Luke reminds his sister that no one's ever really gone, leaving the audience to wonder if he is talking about Kylo Ren's possible redemption, Han Solo's memory, or his own return one day.

"JUDGE ME BY MY SIZE, DO YOU?"

YODA'S WORDS OF WISDOM AND WARNING

WITH NINE-HUNDRED YEARS UNDER HIS TINY BELT, YODA IS THE WISEST OF ALL JEDI MASTERS. HE CERTAINLY PREDICTED ANAKIN SKYWALKER'S EVENTUAL DEMISE. AS YODA TEACHES US LATER, FAILING IS PART OF THE JOB FOR ANY MASTER AND LEARNING FROM THOSE FAILURES IS PERHAPS THE GREATEST LESSON OF ALL.

"FEAR IS THE PATH TO THE DARK SIDE... FEAR LEADS TO ANGER...ANGER LEADS TO HATE...HATE LEADS TO SUFFERING."
(*The Phantom Menace*)

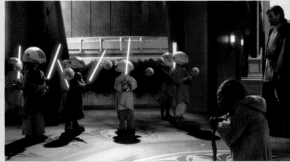

"TRULY WONDERFUL, THE MIND OF A CHILD IS."
(*Attack of the Clones*)

"WHEN NINE HUNDRED YEARS OLD YOU REACH, LOOK AS GOOD YOU WILL NOT."
(*Return of the Jedi*)

"THE GREATEST TEACHER, FAILURE IS."
(*The Last Jedi*)

"LUMINOUS BEINGS
ARE WE... NOT
THIS CRUDE MATTER."

"A JEDI USES THE FORCE FOR
KNOWLEDGE AND DEFENSE,
NEVER FOR ATTACK."

"DO. OR DO NOT.
THERE IS NO TRY."
(*The Empire Strikes Back*)

R2-D2 SAVES THE DAY

ALL THE WAYS R2-D2 HAS RESCUED THE HEROES

WHAT IF THE GREATEST HERO IN THE GALAXY IS ACTUALLY R2-D2? THE EVIDENCE IS MOUNTING THAT THIS LITTLE DROID HAS SAVED VIRTUALLY ALL OTHER CONTENDERS. ACROSS DECADES OF GALACTIC HISTORY, R2-D2 HAS BEEN THERE TO SAVE THE DAY.

ROYAL RESCUE
(*The Phantom Menace*)

When Queen Amidala's starship attempts to break the blockade above Naboo, the ship's hyperdrive takes critical damage. A squad of astromech droids attempts to fix it but only one survives. R2-D2 avoids destruction and receives a royal recognition for his bravery. Little did they know, this wouldn't be the droid's last heroic act.

A

B

FACTORY SHUTDOWN
(*Attack of the Clones*)

Right on time, R2-D2 shuts down the droid factory assembly line on Geonosis to save Padmé Amidala from being covered in molten metal. (**Image A**)

BATTLING DROIDS
(*Revenge of the Sith*)

Droid-on-droid violence ensues during the rescue attempt of Chancellor Palpatine above Coruscant. R2-D2 holds his own against buzz droids who threaten to disassemble Anakin Skywalker's starfighter piece by piece.

TRASH COMPACTOR
(*A New Hope*)

Luke, Han, Leia, and Chewbacca thought the smell was the worst thing about being in the Death Star's trash compactor. That is, until they realized the walls were closing in around them. If not for R2-D2 turning off the compactor remotely, the Rebellion would have been crushed that day. (**Image B**)

HYPERDRIVE HEROICS
(*The Empire Strikes Back*)

As the Rebel heroes attempt to flee Darth Vader at Cloud City, R2-D2 diagnoses and fixes the ship's hyperdrive, foiling Vader's plot by allowing the rebels to fight another day.

ENTER THE EWOKS
(*Return of the Jedi*)

Working with the diminutive Ewoks, R2-D2 lays a trap for the stormtroopers. In the ensuing chaos, the rebel strike team accomplishes their mission to blow up the Imperial shield generator. **(Image C)**

MAP TO SKYWALKER
(*The Force Awakens*)

Deep in his memory banks, R2-D2 holds most of the map that leads the Resistance to Luke Skywalker's hiding place on the planet Ahch-To. Just when the Resistance needs him most, R2 offers up the vital information and joins Rey on her mission to find the old Jedi master. **(Image D)**

PERSUASIVE PROJECTION
(*The Last Jedi*)

Feeling defeated by his previous failures, Luke Skywalker is in no mood to help train another Jedi. R2-D2 changes his mind by showing Luke the holomessage from Leia that started it all: "You're my only hope." **(Image E)**

C-3PO, WORRYWART

LIST OF C-3PO'S FEARS

C-3PO MIGHT BE ABLE TO COMMUNICATE IN SIX MILLION FORMS, BUT HE ISN'T KNOWN FOR HIS BRAVERY. THIS UNLIKELY SIDEKICK NEVER FAILS TO FIND THINGS THAT HE IS AFRAID OF OR MAKE HIS APPREHENSIONS KNOWN.

- BEING SOLO
- MACHINES MAKING MACHINES
- LOSING HIS HEAD
- MEMORY WIPES
- SPACESHIP DESTRUCTION
- THE SPICE MINES OF KESSEL
- UNSAFE ESCAPE PODS
- FROZEN JOINTS
- ROCKY TERRAIN
- JAWAS
- UPSETTING HIS MASTER
- TUSKEN RAIDERS
- SPACE TRAVEL
- UPSETTING A WOOKIEE
- STRANGE COMPUTERS
- BEING LEFT BEHIND
- ASTEROID COLLISIONS
- HEAD ON ATTACKS TOWARD STAR DESTROYERS
- BEING BLASTED INTO PIECES
- UPSETTING JABBA
- KOWAKIAN MONKEY-LIZARD ATTACKS
- GOING AGAINST HIS PROGRAMMING

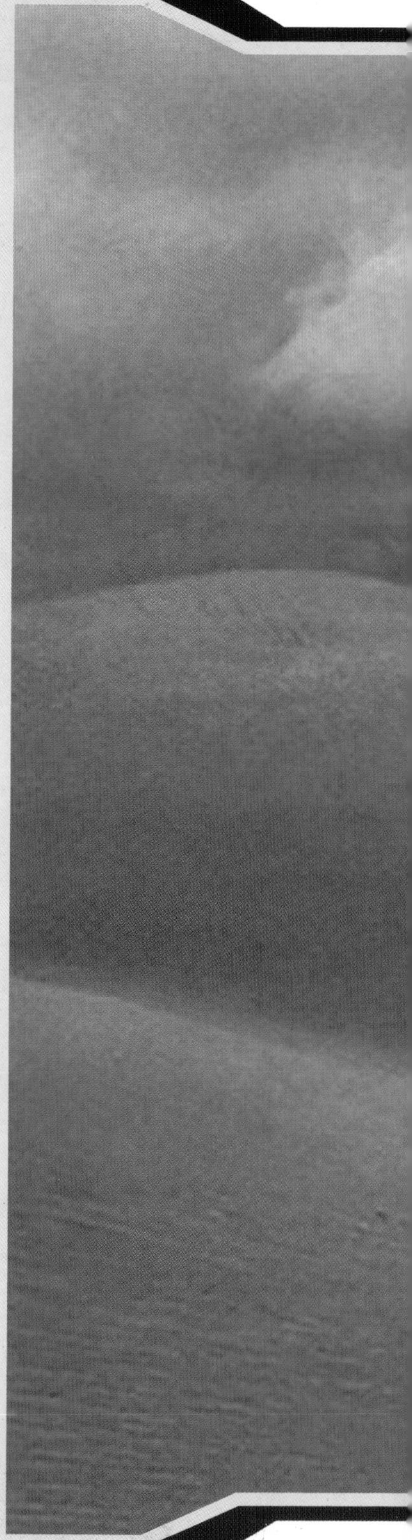

"HELLO, WHAT HAVE WE HERE?"

LANDO CALRISSIAN'S SMOOTHEST MOVES

LANDO CALRISSIAN IS A LOT OF THINGS: SMUGGLER, GAMBLER, REBEL, BUSINESSMAN, AND FRIEND. BUT NO MATTER WHAT ROLE HE'S PLAYING, LANDO IS ALWAYS SMOOTH. THESE ARE THE COOLEST MOVES THIS OLD SMOOTHIE HAS TO OFFER.

SABACC SPORTSMAN
(*Solo: A Star Wars Story*)

Lando's smooth talking helps him con card players the galaxy over. Thanks to a special device on his wrist, Lando ensures he has a winning card up his sleeve at all times. Those around him just assume he's lucky and his winning personality keeps his opponents from suspecting anything. (**Image A**)

THE CALRISSIAN CHRONICLES
(*Solo: A Star Wars Story*)

Even as a young man, Lando believes his years of exploits are worth sharing with the galaxy. Between card games and smuggling missions, he sits down to record his spoken memoirs, known as the Calrissian Chronicles. (**Image B**)

"HELLO, WHAT HAVE WE HERE?"
(*The Empire Strikes Back*)

Leia Organa gets to see first-hand just how smooth Lando can be. Even though she is traveling with Han, Lando doesn't hesitate to lay on the charm. (**Image C**)

IN DISGUISE
(*Return of the Jedi*)

Lando remains calm, cool, and collected as he infiltrates Jabba the Hutt's palace. In disguise as one of Jabba's guards, he waits for the rescue attempt of Han Solo. The disguise itself might look familiar, too. It's the same one that Tobias Beckett used in the heist on Kessel so many years before. (**Image D**)

NOT A SCRATCH
(*Return of the Jedi*)

Han gives Lando the *Millennium Falcon*, at least temporarily, to use in the attack on the second Death Star. Lando promises to return it without a scratch. Though his promise is certainly convincing, he doesn't quite keep his word. In a narrow stretch of the Death Star's interior, Lando clips off the freighter's radar dish.

DANCING WITH EWOKS
(*Return of the Jedi*)

Lando isn't just good with words, he's got some dance moves as well. He shows them off in the well-deserved victory celebration on the forest moon of Endor, where he dances around the campfire with Ewoks and fellow rebels. (**Image E**)

RESCUE ON PASAANA
(*The Rise of Skywalker*)

Lando aids members of the Resistance and helps them evade the First Order.

ACES ARE WILD

TOP PILOTS IN THE GALAXY

Not all *Star Wars* heroes wield lightsabers and use the Force. For these aces, their talents lie behind the controls of a spaceship or starfighter. What they lack in magical abilities, they make up for in bravery and skill.

RIO DURANT
(*Solo: A Star Wars Story*)

Rio is the four-armed pilot and essential member of Tobias Beckett's scoundrel crew. His extra appendages allow him to single-handedly fly ships that normally require two pilots.

BODHI ROOK
(*Rogue One: A Star Wars Story*)

Once a shuttle pilot for the Empire, Bodhi Rook defects to help Galen Erso pass a vital message to the Rebellion. He joins the Rogue One crew on their mission to Scarif, eventually leading to their victory over the Death Star.

WEDGE ANTILLES
(*A New Hope*, *The Empire Strikes Back*, *Return of the Jedi*)

Wedge is either the luckiest or most-skilled pilot in the Rebellion. He is one of the few survivors of the Battle of Yavin, where he flies as Luke Skywalker's wingman against the Death Star. He later pilots a snowspeeder on Hoth as part of Rogue Squadron. At the Battle of Endor, he once again joins an attack on a Death Star, this time as leader of Red Squadron. There he deals one of the final blows to the space station's power core, bringing down the technological terror.

POE DAMERON

(*The Force Awakens, The Last Jedi, The Rise of Skywalker*)

Poe embodies the spirit of an ace pilot. Cocky, bold, and courageous, he is practically fearless in the cockpit. As the Resistance's best pilot, he leads the X-wing attack on Starkiller Base, the defense of D'Qar, and the speeder wing at the Battle of Crait. He's one of the few to survive all three costly battles against the First Order.

NIEN NUNB

(*Return of the Jedi, The Force Awakens, The Last Jedi, The Rise of Skywalker*)

The Sullustan pilot is quietly one of the Rebellion's (and later the Resistance's) most dependable pilots. He famously serves as a co-pilot alongside Lando Calrissian at the Battle of Endor. Years later, he returns to Leia Organa's side as she forms the Resistance.

SNAP WEXLEY

(*The Force Awakens, The Rise of Skywalker*)

A longtime friend and wingman of Poe Dameron, Snap Wexley has a rebellious history that goes back to a young age when he fought against the Empire as a teenager.

TALLISSAN "TALLIE" LINTRA

(*The Last Jedi*)

Lieutenant Tallissan Lintra is a trusted leader in Poe Dameron's Resistance fighter wing. She is his second in command at the Battle of D'Qar, leading the fighter and bomber attack from her A-wing starfighter.

I GOT YOUR BACK

CHARACTERS WHO ARE HANDY IN A FIGHT

WHEN A FIGHT BREAKS OUT, THESE ARE THE CHARACTERS YOU WANT TO HAVE BY YOUR SIDE. EACH BRINGS THEIR OWN UNIQUE SKILLS OR EXPERTISE TO THE BATTLEFIELD. MORE IMPORTANT, EACH IS A LOYAL ALLY TO THEIR FRIENDS AND THOSE THEY HAVE SWORN TO PROTECT.

CHIEFTAN TARFFUL
(*Revenge of the Sith*)

As leader of the Wookiee city of Kachirho, the chieftain personally leads his people into battle to repel the Separatist droid army invasion of Kashyyyk.

TOBIAS BECKETT
(*Solo: A Star Wars Story*)

The scoundrel is a stylish gunslinger who is quick on the trigger. Though you might doubt his loyalty, his skill and experience in matters that require a blaster is unquestionable. (**Image B**)

VAL
(*Solo: A Star Wars Story*)

In Tobias Beckett's ragtag crew of scoundrels, Val is often the voice of reason. When a fight inevitably breaks out, Val's athleticism helps her excel as a saboteur and explosives expert.

CAPTAIN PANAKA
(*The Phantom Menace*)

Panaka is the perceptive, experienced leader of the Naboo security forces sworn to protect the queen. His level-headed demeanor makes him an ideal choice in high-stakes situations. He wields an uncommon savviness in both politics and combat. (**Image A**)

CHIRRUT ÎMWE
(*Rogue One: A Star Wars Story*)

Chirrut's lack of sight makes him no less of a warrior. In close-quarters combat, this former Guardian of the Whills' speed and fluidity catches foes off guard. His heightened senses even allow him to make unlikely blaster shots with his elegant and powerful lightbow weapon. Most of all, his spiritual nature provides a calming effect even during the most stressful situations. (**Image C**)

CASSIAN ANDOR
(*Rogue One: A Star Wars Story*)

A captain in the Rebel Alliance and experienced intelligence officer, Cassian is an unwavering ally to have by your side. He's proven that he will do whatever it takes to complete a mission, including Jyn's fateful attempt to steal the Death Star plans. (**Image D**)

JANNAH
(*The Rise of Skywalker*)

Armed with a bow, Jannah is a skilled warrior and rider. She's unafraid to take on the might of the First Order.

RELUCTANT HEROES

CHARACTERS WHO WOULD RATHER NOT BE IN THE LIMELIGHT

NOT EVERY CHARACTER BEGINS THEIR JOURNEY LOOKING TO BE A HERO. FOR MANY, IT'S A ROLE THAT THEY HESITANTLY GROW INTO. WHILE LUKE SKYWALKER IS OFTEN CONSIDERED A RELUCTANT HERO, HE'S FAR FROM THE ONLY CHARACTER IN THE *STAR WARS* SAGA TO FOLLOW SUCH AN ARC.

JYN ERSO

(*Rogue One: A Star Wars Story*)

After the loss of her parents at the hands of the Empire and being raised by the partisan Saw Gerrera, Jyn Erso isn't looking to join anyone's cause. Her participation with the rebels was meant to be a one-time job, but along the way Jyn rose to the role of leader of Rogue One.

FINN

(*The Force Awakens*, *The Last Jedi*, *The Rise of Skywalker*)

Raised as trooper FN-2187 in the First Order, this former storm-trooper goes on a journey of self-discovery. In the beginning, Finn selfishly seeks to escape the tyranny of the First Order. Then he shifts his loyalties to protecting his new friend Rey, even attempting to leave the Resistance in an effort to save her. His mission to Canto Bight shows that he cares for the greater cause, leading him to rise to the position of hero in the Resistance.

JAR JAR BINKS
(*The Phantom Menace*)

Banished from his home and people, Jar Jar Binks was an unlikely character to unite the Naboo and Gungans. His reluctance to return to the Gungan home city and travel through the dangerous planet core almost kept him from rising to the occasion. Thanks to some convincing by Jedi Qui-Gon Jinn, Binks takes the plunge and becomes a prominent figure in galactic history.

HAN SOLO
(*A New Hope*)

When we meet Han Solo in *A New Hope*, he's only in it for himself (and the money). He has no interest in saving the galaxy or the fledgling Rebellion. He almost walks away from all of it, but thanks to some pressure from his kind-hearted Wookiee co-pilot, he has a last-second change of heart that forever changes his fate. His flying heroics help Luke Skywalker take the shot that destroys the Death Star, forever turning this selfish scoundrel into a rebel hero.

BAZE MALBUS
(*Rogue One: A Star Wars Story*)

Once the most devout member of the Guardians of the Whills, Baze turns into a pragmatic warrior after the destruction of the temple he was sworn to protect. He's a crack shot with a heavy repeater cannon and fiercely loyal to Chirrut and Jyn. Loyalty to his friends, not the cause, inspires him to take part in the rebel mission to steal the Death Star plans.

A B C

BIGGEST BADDIES

THE MAJOR BAD GUYS OF THE *STAR WARS* GALAXY

SINCE 1977, *STAR WARS* HAS GIVEN US ICONIC VILLAINS TO ROOT AGAINST—OR FOR, IF YOU'RE A FAN OF THE DARK SIDE. KNOWN FOR RED-BLADED LIGHTSABERS, EVIL SCHEMES, LIGHTNING SPEWING FROM THEIR FINGERTIPS, OR ARMOR THAT STRIKES FEAR INTO THE VERY HEARTS OF THEIR ENEMIES, THESE WICKED VILLAINS ARE SO GOOD AT BEING SO BAD.

DARTH MAUL
(*The Phantom Menace, Solo: A Star Wars Story*)

This horn-headed Dathomirian Zabrak was the apprentice of the mysterious Sith Lord named Darth Sidious. Armed with a double-bladed red lightsaber, Maul's resilience was legendary. Even after losing his lower half in a lightsaber duel, his hatred and malice kept him alive. (**Image A**)

COUNT DOOKU
(*Attack of the Clones, Revenge of the Sith*)

Once a Jedi Master himself, Count Dooku left the Order and became an apprentice to Darth Sidious. Dooku had the age and wisdom to play both the charismatic Separatist leader and shadowy Sith Lord during the Clone Wars. (**Image B**)

GENERAL GRIEVOUS
(*Revenge of the Sith*)

With cybernetic arms and a metal body, very little remained of Grievous' original form. Driven by his desire to become a superior warrior, his cybernetic upgrades were self-inflicted. Though not a Force-user, Grievous wielded four lightsabers at one time, all collected from the Jedi he defeated. (**Image C**)

DRYDEN VOS
(*Solo: A Star Wars Story*)

As the public face of the notorious gang known as Crimson Dawn, Dryden Vos is proof that villains can also be quite charming. Behind the veil of charisma lies an impatient, cruel man who leaves a path of bodies in his wake. (**Image D**)

G H I

DIRECTOR ORSON KRENNIC

(*Rogue One*)

Calculating and driven, Orson Krennic rose through the Imperial ranks to become Director of Advanced Weapons Research. Tasked with building the Empire's ultimate weapon, Krennic would do anything—or betray anyone—in order to see the Death Star completed. (**Image E**)

DARTH VADER

(*Revenge of the Sith*, *Rogue One*, *A New Hope*, *The Empire Strikes Back*, *Return of the Jedi*)

Once the Jedi Knight Anakin Skywalker, Darth Vader fell to the dark side and became the Emperor's most trusted and dangerous enforcer. Vader was tasked with wiping out all remaining Jedi and later the Rebel Alliance. (**Image F**)

GRAND MOFF TARKIN

(*Rogue One*, *A New Hope*)

A ruthless Imperial bureaucrat and one of Palpatine's most loyal servants, Tarkin oversaw the development of the first Death Star and took control once the battle station was fully operational. Shrewd, merciless, and extremely thorough, Tarkin used the Death Star to destroy worlds in the hope of ultimately crushing the Rebellion. (**Image G**)

EMPEROR PALPATINE

(*Revenge of the Sith*, *The Empire Strikes Back*, *Return of the Jedi*)

Also known as Darth Sidious, Sheev Palpatine plotted for years to overthrow the Republic and declare himself emperor. This seemingly unassuming former politician orchestrated both sides of the Clone Wars, and was master to almost all of the villains on this list. (**Image H**)

KYLO REN

(*The Force Awakens*, *The Last Jedi*, *The Rise of Skywalker*)

Ben Solo, the son of Leia Organa and Han Solo, and once a promising Jedi student of Luke Skywalker, betrayed his parents and his Jedi Order. Obsessed with the legacy of his grandfather, Darth Vader, Ben fell to the dark side and took up the mantle of Kylo Ren. (**Image I**)

SUPREME LEADER SNOKE

(*The Force Awakens*, *The Last Jedi*)

As mysterious as he is evil, Supreme Leader Snoke serves as the leader of the First Order and spiritual mentor to Kylo Ren. Despite his disfigurements, Snoke is exceptionally strong in the Force and foresees that the only threat to his rising power is the Jedi. (**Image J**)

BOBA FETT

(*Attack of the Clones*, *A New Hope*, *The Empire Strikes Back*, *Return of the Jedi*)

The clone son of Jango Fett, Boba grows up to be one of the galaxy's most respected and infamous bounty hunters. Though he is a man of few words, his client list is impressive, working for both the Empire and Jabba the Hutt. (**Image K**)

TWISTED AND EVIL

DARTH VADER'S MOST MEMORABLE LINES

For a shadowy enforcer and a man of few words, Darth Vader makes the most of his limited dialogue. Over the course of the *Star Wars* saga, this Sith Lord has spoken more than a few memorable lines, each more evil than the last.

"BE CAREFUL NOT TO CHOKE ON YOUR ASPIRATIONS, DIRECTOR."
(*Rogue One: A Star Wars Story*)

You don't just ask Vader for a professional recommendation. Orson Krennic's request that Vader tell the Emperor of his good work is met with a Force-choke and a reminder of how dangerous it can be to climb the leadership ladder in the Empire.

"I AM ALTERING THE DEAL. PRAY I DON'T ALTER IT ANY FURTHER."
(*The Empire Strikes Back*)

Lando Calrissian gambled when he made a deal with Vader in order to save Cloud City, but finds himself holding none of the cards. Vader knows he has the upper hand (and military firepower) to get whatever he wants and doesn't hesitate to change the terms of their agreement on the fly.

"NO, *I* AM YOUR FATHER."
(*The Empire Strikes Back*)

Vader corners the young Jedi Luke Skywalker and lets him in on the saga's most shocking secret. In popular culture, the line is often shorthanded as "Luke, I am your father," though that exact phrase is never actually spoken.

"HE WILL JOIN US OR DIE, MY MASTER."
(*The Empire Strikes Back*)

Vader and his master, Darth Sidious, hatch an evil plan to lure Luke Skywalker to the dark side. Vader shows his loyalty to the Sith by declaring he is willing to kill his own son in the name of the cause.

"YOU HAVE FAILED ME FOR THE LAST TIME, ADMIRAL."
(*The Empire Strikes Back*)

Serving as the highest-ranking officer on Vader's flagship is as dangerous as it is prestigious. When Admiral Ozzel commits a series of tactical errors, the Sith Lord makes a statement by killing the officer in front of his replacement.

"IMPRESSIVE . . . MOST IMPRESSIVE."
(*The Empire Strikes Back*)

As Vader and Luke come face-to-face, the Sith Lord is fascinated by the Jedi's potential.

"ONLY YOUR HATRED CAN DESTROY ME."
(*Return of the Jedi*)

Having lured the young Jedi into a fight aboard the Death Star II, all Vader has to do is entice him toward the dark side. He preys on his son's frustration in an attempt to get Luke to tap into his anger.

TEMPER, TEMPER

LIST OF OBJECTS AND PEOPLE DESTROYED BY KYLO REN

KYLO REN'S LEGENDARY ANGER IS NO JOKE. HE HAS A CHIP ON HIS SHOULDER THE SIZE OF A DEATH STAR AND A TEMPER THAT IS FREQUENTLY LOST. THESE ARE THE PEOPLE, PLACES, AND THINGS THAT FELT HIS WRATH.

A

COMMAND BRIDGE
(*The Force Awakens*)

Kylo doesn't take well to bad news. When he learns that Rey and BB-8 have escaped his grasp, he transfers his rage to a nearest computer terminal, hacking and slashing the machine with his lightsaber for no reason other than unbridled anger. (**Image A**)

RESISTANCE STARSHIP HANGAR
(*The Last Jedi*)

Like his grandfather before him, Kylo is quite the pilot. With the Resistance on the run, Ren lays waste to the starship hangar of the Resistance flagship, *Raddus*, with a targeted missile strike. The attack devastates their remaining starfighters leaving the Resistance virtually defenseless.

B

HIS HELMET
(*The Last Jedi*)

After a tough conversation with Supreme Leader Snoke, Kylo takes out his anger on his own helmet. In a rage, he bashes it into pieces. (**Image B**)

SNOKE AND HIS GUARDS
(*The Last Jedi*)

Thinking he can turn Rey to the dark side and rule the galaxy himself, Kylo betrays his own master. With Snoke out of the way, Kylo and Rey must fend off his entire Praetorian Guard, elite warriors who put up quite a fight. (**Image C**)

ALL GROWN UP

CHARACTERS THROUGH THE AGES

THE STORIES TOLD IN *Star Wars* STRETCH THROUGH DECADES OF GALACTIC HISTORY AS WE FOLLOW THE LIVES OF HEROES AND VILLAINS ALIKE. AS TIME MARCHES ON, OUR CHARACTERS CHANGE AND EVOLVE. SOME GROW OLD, SOME TURN EVIL, AND SOME SHOW THE SCARS OF WAR. THIS IS A LOOK AT THOSE CHARACTERS THROUGH THE AGES.

C-3PO
(*The Phantom Menace*
Attack of the Clones
Revenge of the Sith
The Empire Strikes Back
The Force Awakens)

OBI-WAN KENOBI
(*The Phantom Menace*
Attack of the Clones
Revenge of the Sith
A New Hope
Return of the Jedi)

ANAKIN SKYWALKER
(*The Phantom Menace*
Attack of the Clones
Revenge of the Sith
Return of the Jedi)

CHEWBACCA
(*Revenge of the Sith*
Solo: A Star Wars Story
A New Hope
The Force Awakens)

HAN SOLO
(*Solo: A Star Wars Story*
A New Hope
The Force Awakens)

LEIA ORGANA
(*Revenge of the Sith*
A New Hope
The Force Awakens)

LUKE SKYWALKER
(*Revenge of the Sith*
A New Hope
The Force Awakens)

MAUL
(*The Phantom Menace*
Solo: A Star Wars Story)

LANDO CALRISSIAN
(*Solo: A Star Wars Story*
The Empire Strikes Back
The Rise of Skywalker)

KYLO REN
(*The Force Awakens*
The Last Jedi
The Rise of
Skywalker)

NIEN NUNB
(*Return of the Jedi*
The Force Awakens
The Last Jedi)

CHAPTER 2:
PEOPLE, CREATURES, PLACES, AND WORLDS

SMALL BUT MIGHTY

SMALLEST CREATURES

FROM THE CUTE AND CUDDLY PORGS TO THE MANIACAL KOWAKIAN MONKEY-LIZARDS, THESE ARE SOME OF THE SMALLEST CREATURES IN THE GALAXY. BUT DON'T LET THEIR SMALL SIZE FOOL YOU: MANY PLAY QUITE AN IMPORTANT ROLE IN THE STORY OF *STAR WARS*.

PORG

(*The Last Jedi*)

Inquisitive porgs are native to the remote planet Ahch-To. There they nest on the rocky islands that dot the water planet's surface. As cute as they may be, they are also a nuisance known to chew on wiring and upholstery. A group of porgs invaded the *Millennium Falcon* and have become the unlikely companions of Chewbacca. (**Image A**)

GORG

(*The Phantom Menace*)

These small amphibians are regarded as delicacies to Hutts who will eat them alive. Food vendors sell them at markets across the galaxy, often hung by their feet. Gorgs come in a variety of shapes and colors, but are generally identified by their smooth, amphibian skin.

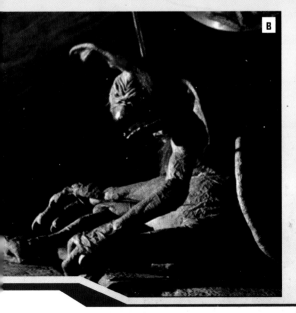

B

NUNA

(*The Phantom Menace*)

Native to the planet Naboo among others, nuna are tiny creatures with leathery skin. This flightless avian species is a popular dish served deep-fried, baked, or as jerky. In some parts of the galaxy, they serve as the ball in a sport fittingly known as "nuna ball."

KOWAKIAN MONKEY-LIZARD

(*Return of the Jedi*)

The cackling laughs of the kowakian monkey-lizards are unmistakable. Jabba the Hutt keeps one as a pet and court jester, named Salacious B. Crumb. They come in a variety of colors and have been known to be sold as pets or even food. (**Image B**)

VULPTEX

(*The Last Jedi*)

Also known to viewers as a crystal fox, these four-legged creatures are native to the desolate planet Crait. They play a pivotal role in saving the Resistance at the Battle of Crait, showing the survivors a way out of the abandoned base. (**Image C**)

19

A FACE ONLY A MOTHER COULD LOVE

UGLIEST CREATURES

Sure, they are ugly, but that doesn't make them any less interesting! These creatures aren't much to look at, but are part of what makes the *Star Wars* galaxy so rich and fascinating.

CORELLIAN HOUND
(*Solo: A Star Wars Story*)

On their home planet of Corellia, hounds serve as guard beasts and trackers for the White Worms, a gang of black market criminals. These snarling creatures keep the young scrumrats in line, making them think twice about betraying their White Worm masters.

WORRT
(*Return of the Jedi*)

Lightning-sharp reflexes and a long tongue help worrts capture unsuspecting prey that wanders too close. Their egg are considered a delicacy and are served in drinks at cantinas throughout the galaxy.

RANCOR
(*Return of the Jedi*)

Rancors are roaring, carnivorous beasts with mangled teeth and monstrous claws. Jabba the Hutt keeps one as a pet in his palace where it feeds on people who displease the gangster. Behind the scenes, the creature's designers thought of the rancor as a cross between a bear and a potato.

HAPPABORE
(*The Force Awakens*)

The four-legged creature with a prominent snout carries cargo on planets like Jakku. They have folds of thick, leathery skin, tiny eyes, and yellowing tusks.

THALA-SIREN
(*The Last Jedi*)

These sea sows are found basking in the sun on the rocky coasts on Ahch-To's islands. Luke Skywalker harvests milk from the docile creatures during his self-imposed exile to the far-flung planet. Their green milk provides him with much-needed nutrition.

20

LIFE-THREATENING CREATURES

THE MOST DANGEROUS CRITTERS IN THE GALAXY

IN A GALAXY TEEMING WITH EXOTIC LIFEFORMS, SOMETHING MUST SIT AT THE TOP OF THE FOOD CHAIN. THESE DANGEROUS CREATURES POSE A REAL DANGER EVEN FOR THE MOST CAPABLE HEROES.

A

SANDO AQUA MONSTER
(*The Phantom Menace*) **(Image A)**

COLO CLAW FISH
(*The Phantom Menace*) **(Image B)**

SUMMA-VERMINOTH
(*Solo: A Star Wars Story*)

MAIRAN
(*Rogue One: A Star Wars Story*)

WAMPA
(*The Empire Strikes Back*) **(Image C)**

SPACE SLUG
(*The Empire Strikes Back*) **(Image D)**

VEXIS SNAKE
(*The Rise of Skywalker*)

21

CREATURE ATTACKS

THE BEST HERO VS. CREATURE MATCHUPS

The *Star Wars* saga is full of monster moments where heroes come face-to-face with vicious creatures. These encounters test their mettle and provide a thrilling distraction from the larger struggle between the forces of good and evil.

OPEE SEA KILLER
(*The Phantom Menace*)

Lurking in the darkest depths, the opee sea killer preys upon the Jedi Qui-Gon Jinn and Obi-Wan Kenobi as they travel by submarine through the watery planet core of Naboo with Jar Jar Binks as their guide. The massive crustacean might have swallowed them whole if not for the fact that it fell prey to an even bigger fish. (**Image A**)

NEXU VS. PADMÉ AMIDALA
(*Attack of the Clones*)

On Geonosis, Padmé, Anakin, and Obi-Wan are captured and face execution at the hands of three vicious beasts. Padmé holds her own against the nexu, a four-eyed creature that attacks its prey with claws and gnarling teeth. Padmé's lockpicking skills and climbing ability allow her to fend off the beast. (**Image B**)

ACKLAY VS. OBI-WAN KENOBI
(*Attack of the Clones*)

Razor-sharp teeth and spear-like claws make the agile acklay a formidable opponent for even a seasoned Jedi Knight like Kenobi. Only after recovering his lightsaber is Obi-Wan able to defeat the beast in the arena of Geonosis. (**Image C**)

DIANOGA VS. LUKE SKYWALKER
(*A New Hope*)

As if being stuck in a trash compactor wasn't bad enough, Luke Skywalker learned that the Empire isn't the only threat on the Death Star. Lurking under the watery surface is a dianoga, a tentacled creature with one eye. The creature might have fed on young Skywalker had it not been scared away by the garbage compactor coming to life. (**Image D**)

SARLACC VS. LANDO CALRISSIAN
(*Return of the Jedi*)

At the executions of Luke, Han, and Chewbacca, it's Lando who finds himself coming closest to death. He nearly falls into the maw of the mighty Sarlacc, a creature that lives in the sands of Tatooine. As the monster tries to pull Lando in with its tentacles, a well-placed blaster shot by Han allows Lando to escape the terrifying encounter. (**Image E**)

RATHTAR VS. FINN
(*The Force Awakens*)

Han and Chewbacca are hauling rathtars when they are cornered by two gangs. In the ensuing scuffle, the rathtars get loose, catching Rey and Finn in the crossfire. One of the creatures catches Finn and nearly swallows him whole, but Rey's quick thinking saves the day. The whole bunch of heroes make their getaway aboard the *Millennium Falcon*, barely escaping the rathtar rampage. (**Image F**)

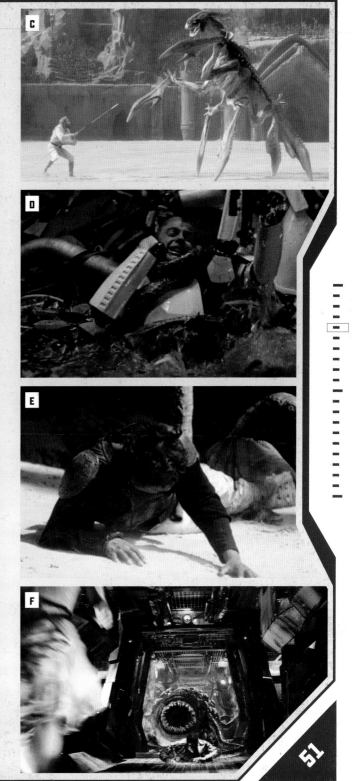

22

SCAVENGING THE GALAXY

GROUPS OR INDIVIDUALS WHO SURVIVE BY SCAVENGING

IT'S NOT MUCH, BUT IT'S A LIVING. THESE BEINGS SUSTAIN THEMSELVES BY SCAVENGING AND TRADING IN SCRAP, OFTEN LEFT BEHIND IN THE WAKE OF WARS AND STRIFE. THEY SHOW ADMIRABLE RESILIENCE AND INGENUITY AS THEY MAKE DO ON SOME OF THE MOST HARSH, DESOLATE PLANETS THE GALAXY HAS TO OFFER.

A

B

JAWAS

(*The Phantom Menace*, *A New Hope*, *Return of the Jedi*)

Hooded cloaks and glowing eyes are the hallmark of Tatooine's Jawas, diminutive scavengers commonly found on the desolate sand planet. They live in moving homes known as sandcrawlers, towering vehicles that house the scraps and machinery they collect. They travel the wastes of Tatooine, searching for material and selling anything of value to the planet's moisture farmers. (**Image A**)

UGNAUGHTS

(*The Empire Strikes Back*)

Living on the lower levels of Cloud City, the hardworking Ugnaughts perform a variety of vital roles to keep the mining operation running. Some work as scavengers, picking through debris in search of valuables that would otherwise be melted into scrap. (**Image B**)

UNKAR PLUTT
(*The Force Awakens*)

Unkar Plutt has a sinister reputation as the junkyard boss of Jakku. Known to other scavengers as the Blobfish, this Crolute trades food rations to other scavengers who bring him salvaged parts from across the planet. His team of thugs help him rule the scavenging trade with an iron fist. (**Image C**)

REY
(*The Force Awakens*)

After being abandoned on Jakku as a girl, Rey ekes out an existence as a scavenger. Like so many others, she barely gets by salvaging the wreckage of Star Destroyers and other military equipment left on the planet after the Battle of Jakku. Rey is an acrobatic explorer, rappelling and climbing to find the most valuable pieces. Anything of value is traded to local boss Unkar Plutt for meager food portions. Rey is proof that great heroes can come from the most humble beginnings. Her resilience and self-determination as a scavenger prove to be vital skills on her journey to become a Jedi. (**Image D**)

CRUSHER ROODOWN
(*The Force Awakens*)

This hulking member of the Abednedo species is one of many scavengers making a living on the planet Jakku. Crusher Roodown was once among the best at his craft before he met the wrath of local boss Unkar Plutt. Plutt's thugs cut off Crusher's arms, which were replaced by pieces of a mechanical load-lifter. (**Image E**)

TEEDO
(*The Force Awakens*)

Short in stature, Teedos are a species native to the desert planet Jakku. Every one of this kind goes by the same name, Teedo. They roam their planet on cybernetically enhanced luggabeasts in search of scrap, of which there is plenty on Jakku. A Teedo attempts to capture BB-8, who might have been sold for scrap had it not been for Rey's intervention. A scavenger herself, she knows how to deal with the likes of a Teedo. (**Image F**)

23

BEASTS OF BURDEN

CREATURES USED FOR ORGANIC TRANSPORT

In a galaxy full of high-tech transportation, these beasts are anything but state of the art. Having adapted to their environments in ways that technology can't, many of these unassuming animals are the perfect transportation for their harsh planets.

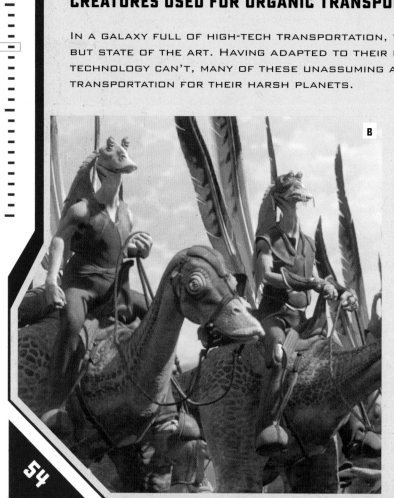

DEWBACK

(*The Phantom Menace*, *A New Hope*)

These plodding reptiles are well accustomed to Tatooine's harsh desert climate. Imperial stormtroopers employ dewbacks during their search for R2-D2 and C-3PO. (**Image A**)

KAADU

(*The Phantom Menace*)

The agile kaadu serve as mounts for Gungan soldiers. Elsewhere in the galaxy, kaadu ribs are a favorite meal. (**Image B**)

RONTO

(*The Phantom Menace*, *A New Hope*)

Towering rontos are a favorite pack animal for Jawas, who fit these beasts with a howdah to carry cargo and passengers alike. (**Image C**)

EOPIE
(*The Phantom Menace*, *Revenge of the Sith*)

As stubborn as they are vital to life on Tatooine, eopies are a common beast of burden for farmers, mechanics, and traders alike.

BANTHA
(*A New Hope*)

Hairy creatures known as banthas serve as livestock and mounts on planets like Tatooine. Thick fur covers nearly every part of their body, except for their ribbed horns and wide lips. The famed blue milk, a drink consumed by farmers and city folk alike, comes from these creatures. (**Image D**)

TAUNTAUN
(*The Empire Strikes Back*)

Rebel soldiers used these two-legged lizards with horns to patrol the icy wastes of Hoth. Though they are native to the planet, even tauntauns can't survive without shelter from the deep freeze of Hoth's nighttime storms. (**Image E**)

FATHIER
(*The Last Jedi*)

These elegant creatures draw huge crowds who love fathier racing. Their powerful legs propel them at great speeds and a pack of fathiers are known to shake the ground as they run. (**Image F**)

ORBAK
(*The Rise of Skywalker*)

Fast and agile, these four-legged animals served as war mounts for Jannah and her gang. (**Image G**)

24

SACRED PLACES

TEMPLES, HISTORIC SITES, AND PLACES WHERE THE FORCE IS STRONG

WHILE THE FORCE FLOWS THROUGH ALL LIVING THINGS, IT IS PARTICULARLY STRONG IN CERTAIN PLACES. THESE TEMPLES, HISTORIC SITES, AND PLANETS ALL SHARE A CONNECTION TO THE FORCE AND PLAY HOST TO IMPORTANT EVENTS IN GALACTIC HISTORY.

A

JEDI TEMPLE

(*The Phantom Menace*, *Attack of the Clones*, *Revenge of the Sith*, *Return of the Jedi*)

This glimmering palace sits high above the city planet of Coruscant, serving as the home to the Jedi Order. Built upon a former Sith shrine, this location has long been a significant site in the ongoing struggle between Jedi and Sith. (**Image A**)

MUSTAFAR

(*Revenge of the Sith*)

This fiery planet's unhappy past and inhospitality makes it a fitting location for Darth Vader's castle.

The Dark Lord's personal residence stands on the site of a Sith Cave, a location he took by force from the local Mustafarians.

JEDHA CITY

(*Rogue One*)

Pilgrims come from across the galaxy to visit this holy city, home to the Temple of Kyber. The city holds sacred value for many of the different religions who believe in the Force. (**Image B**)

B

C

DAGOBAH

(*The Empire Strikes Back,*
Return of the Jedi)

Dagobah might look like a simple swamp, but something about this place holds deeper meaning. Jedi Master Yoda chose the planet for his self-imposed exile, having been mysteriously summoned there years before by the will of the Force. (**Image C**)

AHCH-TO

(*The Force Awakens*, *The Last Jedi*)

On one of the most remote places in the galaxy lies the birthplace of the Jedi Order. This water-covered planet's few rocky islands conceal the first Jedi temple and ancient Jedi texts. Native Lanai maintain the sacred site through the centuries, though it gets few visitors. (**Image D**)

EXEGOL

(*The Rise of Skywalker*)

Hidden away deep in the Unknown Regions of space, steeped in the dark side of the Force, lies the base of the Sith Eternal cult. The planet is almost unreachable due to a swath of nearly unnavigable space.

D

25

HOME BASES

HQ AND BASES OF THE REBEL ALLIANCE AND RESISTANCE

As the scrappy underdogs in the fight between good and evil, the Rebel Alliance (and later the Resistance) must conduct their struggle from hidden bases and modest headquarters. From their home base, they make the most of their limited resources while staying hidden from their more powerful enemies until the time is right.

A

YAVIN 4
(*Rogue One*, *A New Hope*)

On the jungle moon of Yavin 4, the Rebel Alliance makes their headquarters in the ruins of the Great Temple. Its stone-paved landing pads and cavernous interior makes it the perfect location for the fledgling alliance's growing fleet of starfighters. It is from this base that the Alliance wins its first major victory against the Galactic Empire and where they analyze the plans to the Death Star battle station to find its weakness. (**Image A**)

HOTH
(*The Empire Strikes Back*)

The ice planet of Hoth is home to Echo Base, the subterranean headquarters of the Rebel Alliance after the Battle of Yavin. While its remote location is a strategic advantage, the harsh conditions are a constant challenge for the rebels. They must specially modify their equipment for the extreme cold and enlist native creatures like tauntauns for travel. (**Image B**)

B

HOME ONE
(*Return of the Jedi*)

This MC80 star cruiser is more than just the flag-ship of Admiral Ackbar; it served as the mobile headquarters during the later years of the Rebel Alliance's struggle against the Empire. The briefing room plays host to Alliance leadership as they make final preparations for the Battle of Endor, paving the way for the destruction of the second Death Star and the end of Emperor Palpatine's rule. (**Image C**)

D'QAR
(*The Force Awakens*, *The Last Jedi*)

When General Leia Organa organized a small force to combat the growing threat of the First Order, they make their headquarters in a familiar fashion. They find D'Qar the perfect location to hide under-ground, as the hangars there provide protection and accessibility for launching their starfighters. The command room bustles with activity, just as similar ones did during the time of the Rebellion against the Empire. (**Image D**)

CRAIT
(*The Last Jedi*)

The salt-covered Outer Rim planet of Crait served as a base for both the Rebellion and Resistance. The rebels took up residence in the sturdy old mines that provided protection against bombardment. Decades later, Leia and the surviving members of the Resistance made a stand at the abandoned base, holding out long enough to be rescued by Rey. (**Image E**)

AJAN KLOSS
(*The Rise of Skywalker*)

Scouted as a potential landing spot for the Rebel Alliance during the time of the Galactic Civil War, this verdant planet, covered in jungles, served as the base for the struggling Resistance. It was there that Rey continued her Jedi training, under the guidance of General Leia Organa. (**Image F**)

26

PLACES OF SCUM AND VILLAINY

CENTERS OF UNDERWORLD ACTIVITY

THE MOS EISLEY CANTINA IS JUST ONE OF MANY PLACES WHERE SCOUNDRELS, SMUGGLERS, SLAVERS, CRIMINALS, AND GANGSTERS FREQUENT. WATCH YOUR STEP, THESE CENTERS OF UNDERWORLD ACTIVITY CAN BE A LITTLE ROUGH.

OUTLANDER CLUB

(*Attack of the Clones*)

Far from the gleaming surface of the city planet Coruscant, the Outlander Club is a nightclub and gambling establishment with a sinister reputation. Disreputable beings gather here for entertainment, some even partaking in the use of illegal death sticks sold by dishonest dealers. (**Image A**)

THE LODGE AT FORT YPSO

(*Solo: A Star Wars Story*)

In the remote outpost of Fort Ypso on the icy planet Vandor, the Lodge served as the center of activity for the small village. It housed an illegal droid fighting ring, a saloon, and gambling tables. All do their part to attract unsavory characters.

KESSEL

(*Solo: A Star Wars Story*)

The planet Kessel is known for its spice mines, brutal operations that run on slave labor. Spice is an addicting drug that has terrible effects on its users, but is a vital part of the Pyke Syndicate's criminal empire. They run the mines here, working Wookiee slaves to the death in their pursuit of riches. (**Image B**)

MOS EISLEY CANTINA

(*A New Hope*)

Tatooine's Mos Eisley Cantina is a notoriously rough place. It's the kind of joint where someone can lose an arm or get blasted and the other customers barely take notice. But as a hangout for pilots, it's the best place in this corner of the desert planet.

JABBA THE HUTT'S PALACE

(*Return of the Jedi*)

The gangster Jabba holds court in this sprawling desert castle. The palace is crawling with denizens as he surrounds himself with entertainers, staff, bounty hunters, and seedy friends at all times.

MAZ'S CASTLE

(*The Force Awakens*)

The pirate queen Maz Kanata plays host to smugglers and scoundrels of all kinds in her ancient castle. A giant statue of Maz welcomes guests. This refuge had only one rule: no fighting. (**Image C**)

CANTO BIGHT CASINO

(*The Last Jedi*)

A popular destination for the galaxy's most affluent citizens, Canto Bight might not look like a shady place on the surface, but look further and you'll find it has a dark secret. There's only one way to get this rich: selling arms to the highest bidders. The people at Canto Bight enjoy the finest luxuries, paid for in blood money. (**Image D**)

THIEVES' QUARTER OF KIJIMI

(*The Rise of Skywalker*)

Located on a frigid planet in the Mid Rim, the Thieves' Quarter is comprised of monasteries that became home to all manner of scoundrels, smugglers, and other nefarious characters. Those who came here generally preferred to stay hidden from the rest of the galaxy.

27

HIDDEN HOMES

CHARACTER HOMES THAT ARE PURPOSEFULLY HARD TO FIND

THOUGH NOT EXACTLY A JEDI TRADITION, SOME OF THE MOST LEGENDARY JEDI HAVE FOLLOWED IN THEIR MASTERS' FOOTSTEPS BY GOING INTO HIDING IN TIMES OF CRISIS. YODA, OBI-WAN KENOBI, AND EVEN LUKE SKYWALKER HAVE ALL SOUGHT SHELTER WHILE BEING HUNTED BY MEMBERS OF THE DARK SIDE. THEY, AND OTHERS, SEEK REFUGE IN HOMES AND LOCATIONS THAT ARE PURPOSEFULLY HARD TO FIND.

A

OTOH GUNGA
(*The Phantom Menace*)

A hidden city below a lake on Naboo, Otoh Gunga is the capital of the aquatic Gungan species. There they live in bubble-like structures that provide a network of dry, breathable living spaces far from the gaze of the Naboo people living on the planet's surface. (**Image A**)

DEN OF THE WHITE WORMS
(*Solo: One A Star Wars Story*)

Underground lairs are good for criminals and great for aliens whose skin burns in sunlight. Lady Proxima and her fellow Grindalids rule their crime ring from this dark headquarters, hidden in the depths of Corellia. (**Image B**)

B

SAW GERRERA'S BASE
(*Rogue: One A Star Wars Story*)
Saw's Rebel Partisans strike from this underground militia base on the holy moon of Jedha. Fueled by Gerrera's paranoia, the base's location is a tightly held secret requiring that all outsiders be blindfolded before arrival.

BEN KENOBI'S HUT
(*A New Hope*)
During his time in hiding on Tatooine Obi-Wan Kenobi assumes the name Ben Kenobi and takes up residence in a secluded hut out beyond the Dune Sea. **(Image C)**

YODA'S HUT
(*The Empire Strikes Back*, *Return of the Jedi*)
Yoda's exile after the fall of the Galactic Republic takes him to the swamp planet of Dagobah. From there, he stays in touch with the Force, awaiting the eventual arrival of Luke Skywalker for his Jedi training. While Dagobah is not the most hospitable planet, it has a mysteriously strong connection to the Force. **(Image D)**

LUKE'S HUT
(*The Last Jedi*)
The planet Ahch-To is said to be the birthplace of the Jedi Order. If Luke Skywalker had his way, it would have been the location of the end of the Jedi, too. After his attempt to train the next generation of Jedi fails, Luke exiles himself to one of the most hidden places in the galaxy where he seeks to live out his final days in a hut near the first Jedi temple. **(Image E)**

28

EXTREME LIVING

PLANETS WITH THE HARSHEST ENVIRONMENTS

LIFE ISN'T EASY ON THESE EXTREME PLANETS. THEY EXHIBIT HARSH
ENVIRONMENTS OR SEVERE FEATURES THAT CHALLENGE OUR HEROES. THE BEINGS
WHO LIVE THERE LEARN TO ADAPT, OFTEN CREATING CITIES THAT ARE AS UNIQUE
AS THE PLANETS ON WHICH THEY ARE BUILT.

A

KAMINO
(*Attack of the Clones*)
Torrential rains and crashing waves might seem like
an unlikely place to find some of the galaxy's finest
scientists, but it is here that the cloners of Kamino
built their factories. They live and work in towering
cities, built atop stilts high above the water-covered
surface. (**Image A**)

UTAPAU
(*Revenge of the Sith*)
Utapau is covered in grassy plains marked with
immense sinkholes. Most of its inhabitants make
their homes carved into the walls of the sinkholes,
finding refuge from the harsh winds that make life
challenging on the surface. (**Image B**)

CATO NEIMOIDIA
(*Revenge of the Sith*)
Massive rock arches and spires rise up from the
surface of Cato Neimoidia, whose surface is covered in acidic oceans. The native Neimoidians
construct massive bridges where whole cities hang
suspended in the air.

B

C

D

MUSTAFAR

(*Revenge of the Sith*, *Rogue One: A Star Wars Story*)

Waterfalls of lava, seas of melted ore, and exploding geysers create extreme conditions across Mustafar. Native Mustafarians have adapted to life in underground caverns on a planet where few others can survive. (**Image C**)

KESSEL

(*Solo: A Star Wars Story*)

Kessel's rocky surface is dotted with caustic pools. Making matters worse, the primary industry is spice mining, a business built upon the backs of slave laborers. The slaves live their lives deep underground in mine shafts overseen by ruthless criminal syndicates.

MIMBAN

(*Solo: A Star Wars Story*)

Thick clouds, heavy rains, dense mud and tenacious natives make Mimban a dreadful battlefield during the Clone Wars and Imperial era alike. The battles here stretch on for seemingly an eternity as combat is bogged down by the harsh conditions.

HOTH

(*The Empire Strikes Back*)

This ice and snow-covered planet gets so cold at night that most lifeforms freeze to death. Frequent meteor strikes and predatory beasts only make it less hospitable. (**Image D**)

CRAIT

(*The Last Jedi*)

White salt fields stretch as far as the eye can see on Crait, concealing red soil underneath. Deep beneath the surface lie massive crystal caverns, large enough to fly a small freighter through.

CANTONICA

(*The Last Jedi*)

Don't mistake the luxurious casino city of Canto Bight for the rest of Cantonica. The lush town sits amid an artificial ocean on a largely desolate desert planet.

KEF BIR

(*The Rise of Skywalker*)

One of the nine satellites orbiting Endor, this oceanic world was to be an Imperial sanctuary, before the Empire decided it was too unsuitable for its purposes. After the destruction of the second Death Star, the world became toxic and littered with debris, including a section of the battle station that plunged into the ocean. (**Image E**)

E

29

CITIES THAT NEVER SLEEP

PLANETS WITH THE LIVELIEST CITIES OR WHERE THE WHOLE PLANET IS ONE CITY

WHILE MANY PLANETS IN *STAR WARS* HAVE TOWNS AND VILLAGES, SOME ARE PARTICULARLY KNOWN FOR THEIR NOTEWORTHY CITIES. THESE ARE SOME OF THE MOST EPIC AND UNIQUE PLACES THE VAST GALAXY HAS TO OFFER.

CORUSCANT

(*The Phantom Menace*, *Attack of the Clones*, *Revenge of the Sith*, *Return of the Jedi*)

Coruscant is one giant urban center covering the entire planet. Over the millennia, the city has grown upon itself, rising thousands of levels high. The highest levels now form the surface of the planet and are inhabited by the most elite members of Coruscant society. **(Image A)**

NABOO

(*The Phantom Menace*, *Attack of the Clones*, *Revenge of the Sith*, *Return of the Jedi*)

The capital city Theed is a majestic metropolis befitting the peaceful elegance of Naboo's culture. At the center stands the Palace Plaza, a serene cliffside palace that serves as home of the Naboo royalty.

A

B

CORELLIA
(*Solo: A Star Wars Story*)
Corellia is best known for its starship manufacturing and the center of that industry can be found on the planet's capital, Coronet City. In the time of the Empire, the shipyards there work day and night producing Star Destroyers and other vessels for the massive Imperial Starfleet.

RING OF KAFRENE
(*Rogue One: A Star Wars Story*)
The Ring of Kafrene isn't a planet, but rather a city that holds together two planetoids in the Kafrene asteroid belt. This mazelike structure serves as both mining colony and trading post whose crowded streets play host to any number of shady inhabitants.

CLOUD CITY
(*The Empire Strikes Back*)
Floating among the clouds around the planet Bespin, Cloud City is the stylish community under the watch of its Baron Administrator, Lando Calrissian. The primary industry is tibanna gas mining, which it harvests and refines from the nearby gas giant. Its industrial function is well concealed by the sophisticated lifestyle experienced by most of its citizens who enjoy beautiful vistas and relative peace during the Galactic Civil War. (**Image B**)

HOSNIAN PRIME
(*The Force Awakens*)
This cosmopolitan planet whose cities host massive skyscrapers is best known as the capital of the New Republic. The urban sprawl around the capital is large enough to be seen from space, covering much of the surface of the planet.

CANTONICA
(*The Last Jedi*)
The galaxy's most wealthy citizens escape to the casino city of Canto Bight, an artificial oasis built on the planet Cantonica. The lively celebration of wealth attracts some of the most unscrupulous members of galactic high society, including arms dealers who earn their fortunes on the back of war and suffering. Here they find rest, relaxation, and entertainment to fit any species or taste. (**Image C**)

C

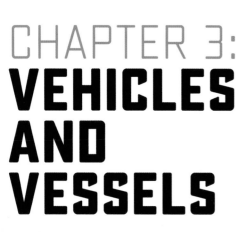

CHAPTER 3:
VEHICLES
AND
VESSELS

30

NAME THAT TIE FIGHTER

VARIATIONS OF THE FEARSOME STARFIGHTER

WITH DISTINCTIVE EYEBALL COCKPITS, PROMINENT WINGS, AND THE TERRIFYING HOWL OF THEIR TWIN ION ENGINES, THE TIE FIGHTER IS THE ICONIC STARFIGHTER OF THE EMPIRE. WHILE THE TIE/IN IS THE MOST COMMON VARIANT, THE EMPIRE BUILT MANY SPECIALIZED VARIATIONS TO FILL UNIQUE ROLES IN THE IMPERIAL NAVY. DECADES LATER, THE FIRST ORDER IMPROVES UPON THE CLASSIC TIE DESIGNS TO CREATE EVEN MORE CAPABLE VARIANTS FOR THEIR OWN CONQUEST OF THE GALAXY. THESE ARE ALL OF THE MAJOR VARIANTS.

TIE FIGHTER
(*Solo: A Star Wars Story,*
Rogue One:
A Star Wars Story,
A New Hope,
The Empire Strikes Back,
Return of the Jedi) (**Image A**)

TIE BOMBER
(*The Empire Strikes Back,*
Return of the Jedi) (**Image B**)

DARTH VADER'S TIE ADVANCED X1
(*A New Hope*) (**Image C**)

TIE INTERCEPTOR
(*Return of the Jedi*) (**Image D**)

TIE STRIKER
(*Rogue One: A Star Wars Story*) (**Image E**)

TIE REAPER
(*Rogue One: A Star Wars Story*) (**Image F**)

TIE BRUTE
(*Solo: A Star Wars Story*)
(**Image G**)

SPECIAL FORCES TIE FIGHTER
(*The Force Awakens*)
(**Image H**)

TIE WHISPER
(*The Rise of Skywalker*)
(**Image I**)

A

B

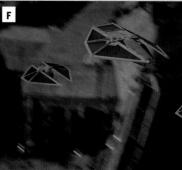

F

H

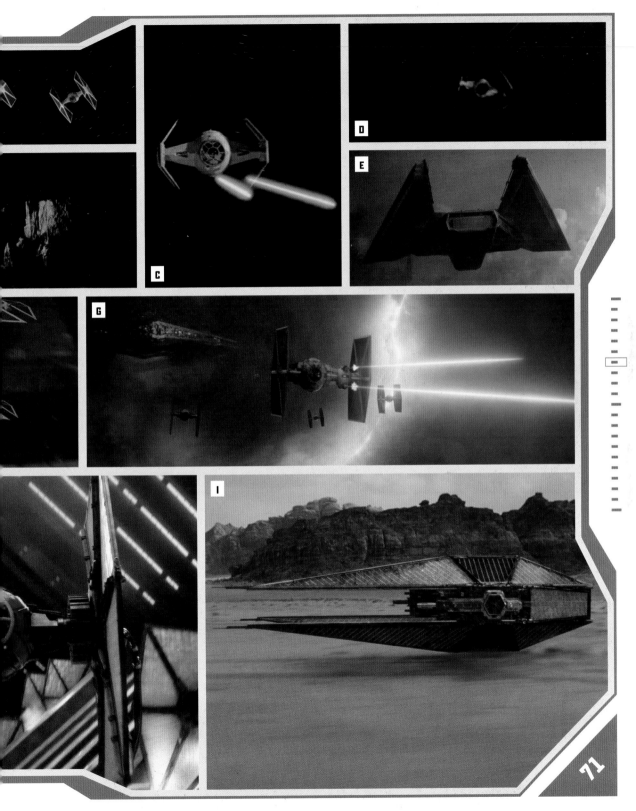

C

D

E

G

I

31

TRICKED-OUT SHIPS

THE MOST UPDATED AND SPECIALIZED VESSELS

As if flying through space at lightspeed wasn't enough, *Star Wars* is full of specially upgraded vessels that push the limits of galactic technology. These exceptional ships and vessels are as unique as the characters who fly them.

PODRACERS
(*The Phantom Menace*)

Fast, dangerous, and illegal, podracing is a popular sport that tests the limits of the racing pods, their pit crews, and pilots alike. Though they share similar features, each podracer is a custom-built creation, often reflecting the style and personality of the owner. (**Image A**)

A

SCIMITAR
(*The Phantom Menace*)

Darth Maul's personal vessel, also known as the Sith Infiltrator, is equipped with a rare cloaking system to allow the shadowy apprentice to move through the galaxy without catching the attention of the Jedi. (**Image B**)

NABOO ROYAL STARSHIP
(*The Phantom Menace*)

The J-type 327 Nubian starship is a fitting ship for the Queen of Naboo. This peaceful ship isn't outfitted with weapons and instead sports advanced deflector shields for protection. Its most defining feature is the sleek, hand-crafted chromium hull. (**Image C**)

SLAVE I
(*Attack of the Clones, The Empire Strikes Back*)

Jango Fett's legacy lives on not only through his son, Boba, but in his highly modified attack and patrol craft. Pursuing enemies are in for an explosive surprise when they discover one of the many systems upgrades includes seismic charges dropped behind the ship. (**Image D**)

B

C

D

E

F

G

HAN'S *FALCON*

(*A New Hope*, *The Empire Strikes Back*, *Return of the Jedi*, *The Force Awakens*, *The Last Jedi*, *The Rise of Skywalker*)

When Han Solo takes ownership of the *Millennium Falcon*, he outfits it with his own customization. Unlike Lando, Han isn't looking for stylish upgrades. Instead, the smuggler favors equipment that boosts the ship's raw performance, no matter the aesthetic consequences. Upgraded military-grade cannons are particularly necessary for all of the tough spots in which Han finds himself over the years. (**Image H**)

ANAKIN'S ETA-2 JEDI STARFIGHTER

(*Revenge of the Sith*)

A tinkerer since a young age, even as a Jedi Knight, Anakin Skywalker finds ways to upgrade the Jedi starfighter he flies during the later stages of the Clone Wars. (**Image E**)

LANDO'S *FALCON*

(*Solo: A Star Wars Story*)

Lando Calrissian's sense of style extends to his Corellian YT-1300 freighter, the *Millennium Falcon*. He makes it his own, inside and out, balancing beauty with performance. The auxiliary craft added to the ship's bow gives it a streamlined look not found on stock models. (**Image F**)

U-WING

(*Rogue One: A Star Wars Story*)

The troop transport of the Rebel Alliance specializes in deploying troops into battlefields, foregoing dogfighting ability for troop capacity and air-to-ground gunnery turrets to clear landing zones. (**Image G**)

EMPEROR'S SHUTTLE

(*Return of the Jedi*)

Visually, there is little to differentiate Emperor Palpatine's shuttle from the rest. Aside from a stripe down the cockpit of the craft, it looks like any other. What sets it apart is the rare tech it carries, including a cloaking device. (**Image I**)

BLACK ONE

(*The Force Awakens*, *The Last Jedi*)

Poe Dameron's X-wing sports an upgraded engine booster pod in *The Last Jedi*, helping the ace pilot dodge First Order capital ship defenses. (**Image J**)

H

I

J

32

WALK OR CRAWL

THE BIGGEST, TALLEST, AND TOUGHEST LAND VEHICLES

While the Trade Federation's Armored Assault Tank is bristling with weapons, its size pales in comparison to the vehicles that come later. The Empire (and later the First Order) expands on the walkers of the Republic era to build ever more imposing land vehicles to crush any resistance that stands before them. These are the most impressive land vehicles.

AT-M6
(*The Last Jedi*)
36.18 meters

AT-ACT
(*Rogue One:
A Star Wars Story*)
31.85 meters

MTT TRANSPORT
(*The Phantom Menace*)
10.54 meters

AT-TE
(*Attack of the Clones,
Revenge of the Sith*)
9.57 meters

**ARMORED ASSAULT
TANK (AAT)**
(*The Phantom Menace*)
4.3 meters

AT-AT
(*The Empire
Strikes Back,
Return of the Jedi*)
22.5 meters

HAVW A6 JUGGERNAUT
(*Revenge of the Sith,
Rogue One: A Star Wars Story*)
30.4 meters

33

BEST OF THE REST

OTHER SIGNIFICANT VESSELS

These noteworthy vessels represent a diverse array of factions, roles, and purposes. What they share in common is the important role they play in the story of *Star Wars*. These ships both big and small drive the action forward, carry heroes and villains into battle, and have become iconic in their own right.

JEDI STARFIGHTER

(*Attack of the Clones*)

The wedge-shaped starfighter of the Jedi shares the shape of the Imperial Star Destroyer, foreshadowing the fall of the Republic into dictatorship. (**Image A**)

X-WING

(*Rogue One: A Star Wars Story*, *A New Hope*, *The Empire Strikes Back*, *Return of the Jedi*, *The Force Awakens*, *The Last Jedi*)

The nimble starship is synonymous with heroics, having brought down two Death Stars and Starkiller Base. (**Image B**)

Y-WING

(*Rogue One: A Star Wars Story*, *A New Hope*, *Return of the Jedi*, *The Rise of Skywalker*)

A rugged fighter-bomber, Y-wings can take down a Star Destroyer in the right hands. (**Image C**)

STAR DESTROYER

(*Rogue One*, *A New Hope*, *The Empire Strikes Back*, *Return of the Jedi*)

Star Destroyers are the preeminent symbol of Imperial might.

TANTIVE IV

(*A New Hope*)

The first starship ever seen in a *Star Wars* film; this blockade runner carried Princess Leia in possession of the Death Star plans as she fled from Darth Vader.

SNOWSPEEDER

(*The Empire Strikes Back*)

Atmospheric snowspeeders were the last line of defense for the rebels at the Battle of Hoth. Using tow cables, they could wrap the legs of AT-AT walkers. (**Image D**)

SUPER STAR DESTROYER

(*The Empire Strikes Back*, *Return of the Jedi*)

What's better than a Star Destroyer? A Super Star Destroyer. Darth Vader's flagship dwarfs other Imperial battleships, stretching on for kilometers.

SUPREMACY

(*The Last Jedi*)

The flagship of Supreme Leader Snoke is the mobile headquarters for the First Order, complete with factories, training facilities, and permanent crew quarters. (**Image E**)

RADDUS

(*The Last Jedi*)

Leia Organa's mobile flagship is equipped with experimental deflector shields that allow it to withstand long-range bombardment from the *Supremacy* until the dwindling fuel supply runs out. Vice Admiral Holdo sacrifices the ship—and herself—to allow Organa and the rest of the Resistance to get away. (**Image F**)

MG-100 STARFORTRESS SF-17

(*The Last Jedi*)

Resistance bombers pay a heavy price in order to destroy a First Order Siege Dreadnought at the Battle of D'Qar. Their sacrifice allows the rest of the Resistance to fight on another day. (**Image G**)

34

STICKING THE LANDING

TYPES OF LANDING GEAR AND DIFFERENT WAYS SHIPS CAN LAND

In the *Star Wars* galaxy, even something as seemingly simple as landing can prove to be quite complicated. With exotic ship designs like these, the way they stay put is almost as interesting as how they fly through space.

NABOO N-1 STARFIGHTER
(*The Phantom Menace*, *Attack of the Clones*)

The sleek lines of the N-1 Starfighter aren't just for graceful looks. The pointed end of the ship plugs into the wall of the Royal hangar when not in use.

VULTURE DROID STARFIGHTER
(*The Phantom Menace*, *Revenge of the Sith*)

These Trade Federation fighters transform into miniature walkers, allowing them to stride around hangars and cling to the surface of capital ships. **(Image A)**

SLAVE I
(*Attack of the Clones*, *The Empire Strikes Back*)

In flight, Boba Fett's inherited patrol craft flies upright with its heavy blaster cannons and cockpit facing forward. To land, it lies on its stern with the cockpit facing up.

SOULLESS ONE
(*Revenge of the Sith*)

When General Grievous's craft lands, the thrust vectoring fin at the back of it lifts out of the way to allow the rear landing gear to extend.

FIRST LIGHT
(*Solo: A Star Wars Story*)

The criminal leader Dryden Vos travels the galaxy in a luxurious Kalevalan yacht. It flies upright and generally doesn't land, instead hovering near its mooring to allow passengers to board. **(Image B)**

DELTA-CLASS T-3C SHUTTLE
(*Rogue One: A Star Wars Story*)

The long wings of Imperial Director Orson Krennic's shuttle not only fold upward when the ship lands, their extensive surface area houses advanced antennae that allow for deep-space communication.

FIRST ORDER TIE FIGHTER
(*The Force Awakens*, *The Last Jedi*, *The Rise of Skywalker*)

When not in use aboard First Order Star Destroyers, their TIE fighters are stacked neatly in vertical rows and conveyed from storage to the flight deck when needed. **(Image C)**

UPSILON-CLASS COMMAND SHUTTLE
(*The Force Awakens*, *The Last Jedi*)

When landing, the tall wings of Kylo Ren's shuttle retract to half their height, protecting the long-range sensor arrays housed there in more durable armor.

A

B

C

35

THE NEED FOR SPEED

THE FASTEST LAND SPEEDERS AND BIKES

THOUGH THEIR GENERAL DESIGNS ARE GROUNDED IN REAL-WORLD TECHNOLOGY (CARS AND MOTORCYCLES), THE LANDSPEEDERS AND SPEEDERBIKES IN *STAR WARS* ARE FASTER AND MORE AGILE THAN ANY GROUND VEHICLES ON OUR PLANET. THESE ARE SOME OF THE FASTEST THE GALAXY HAS TO OFFER.

SINGLE TROOPER AERIAL PLATFORM (STAP)
(*The Phantom Menace*)
400 km/h

GENERAL GRIEVOUS' TSMEU-6 WHEEL BIKE
(*Revenge of the Sith*)
330 km/h

200 KM/H	250 KM/H	300 KM/H	350 KM/H	400 KM/H

C-PH PATROL SPEEDER BIKE
(*Solo: A Star Wars Story*)
400km/h

LUKE SKYWALKER'S X-34 LANDSPEEDER
(*A New Hope*)
250 km/h

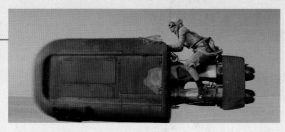

REY'S SPEEDER
(*The Force Awakens*)
425 km/h

BLOODFIN
(*The Phantom Menace*)
650 km/h

450 KM/H	500 KM/H	550 KM/H	600 KM/H	650 KM/H

ENFYS NEST'S MODIFIED CAELII-MERCED SKYBLADE-330
(*Solo: A Star Wars Story*)
600 km/h

36

"STOP THAT SHIP!"

LIST OF STOLEN SHIPS

SOMETIMES OUR HEROES MUST RESORT TO THIEVERY IN THE NAME OF THEIR MISSION. BUT WHEN THE FATE OF THE GALAXY IS AT STAKE, WHO CAN BLAME THEM? THESE ARE THE CRAFTS THE HEROES HAVE STOLEN FOR THE SAKE OF A CAUSE.

A

ANAKIN'S XJ-6 SPEEDER

(*Attack of the Clones*)

While chasing down the assassin Zam Wesell through the skies of Coruscant, Anakin commandeers this hot rod of an airspeeder. Even a Jedi must resort to theft in extreme circumstances. (**Image A**)

ZETA-CLASS CARGO SHUTTLE

(*Rogue One: A Star Wars Story*)

Thanks to the know-how of defector pilot Bodhi Rook and a stolen Imperial cargo shuttle, the members of the Rogue One team infiltrate one of the Empire's most secretive facilities on their successful mission to steal the Death Star plans.

M-68 LANDSPEEDER

(*Solo: A Star Wars Story*)

Han Solo's skills as a pilot and driver first reveal themselves on the dangerous streets of Corellia, where a young Han manages to hotwire a landspeeder from some criminals

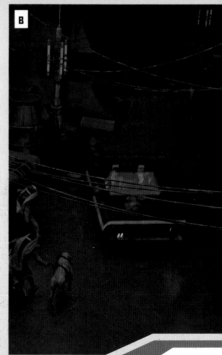

B

he was trying to scam. He managed to get away with his life and the speeder, but his scheme was shortsighted. The ordeal put him at odds with his crime boss, Lady Proxima. (**Image B**)

MILLENNIUM FALCON

(*Solo: A Star Wars Story*, *A New Hope*, *The Empire Strikes Back*, *Return of the Jedi*, *The Force Awakens*, *The Last Jedi*, *The Rise of Skywalker*)

Rey and Finn steal the *Millennium Falcon* on Jakku, adding their names to a long list of the ship's thieves. Before Rey took it, junk dealer Unkar Plutt held the vessel, which he stole from the Irving boys who themselves lifted it from gunrunner Gannis Ducain.

IMPERIAL SPEEDER BIKE

(*Return of the Jedi*)

When Luke and Leia steal an Imperial 74-Z speeder bike on Endor, they end up on a high-speed chase against scout troopers. Flying just feet above the ground at hundreds of kilometers an hour through the heavily wooded forest makes for a thrilling, but short, encounter. (**Image C**)

LIBERTINE

(*The Last Jedi*)

Scoundrel DJ and BB-8 team up to escape Canto Bight by stealing a luxury staryacht known as the *Libertine*. Pilfering such a ship doesn't weigh on one's conscious quite so much when you consider the ship is owned by a filthy rich war profiteer.

TYDIRIUM

(*Return of the Jedi*)

Rebel heroes led by Han Solo fly right under the nose of the Imperial Starfleet thanks to the stolen shuttle (and matching clearance codes). Chewbacca's casual flying leads the strike team to the forest moon of Endor and eventually the defeat of the second Death Star. (**Image D**)

CHAPTER 4:
TECHNOLOGY
AND CULTURE

37

DISTINGUISHED DROIDS

NOBLE DROIDS (THAT AREN'T R2-D2 OR C-3PO)

WHEN YOU THINK ABOUT NOTABLE DROIDS FROM *STAR WARS*, FUSSY PROTOCOL DROID C-3PO AND HIS ASTROMECH COUNTERPART R2-D2 PROBABLY COME TO MIND. BUT THERE ARE OTHER DROIDS WHO MAKE A DIFFERENCE IN THE GALAXY, EACH WITH THEIR OWN UNIQUE SKILLS, QUIRKS, AND PERSONALITIES.

K-2SO

(*Rogue One: A Star Wars Story*)

K-2SO was once an Imperial security droid until reprogrammed by rebel agent Cassian Andor. He serves as both pilot and muscle and benefits from the added ability to blend in at Imperial bases during intelligence missions. His reprogramming creates a peculiar personality that can catch others by surprise, but his loyalty to his friends is unquestionable.

BB-8

(*The Force Awakens*, *The Last Jedi*, *The Rise of Skywalker*)

The astromech droid BB-8 is the loyal sidekick and copilot of Poe Dameron. Unlike many astromechs in Resistance service, he does far more than just repair Dameron's X-wing starfighter. Poe entrusts a map to the location of Luke Skywalker in BB-8's care on Jakku, counting on the little droid to safeguard the hopes of the Resistance.

C1-10P, CHOPPER
(*Rogue One: A Star Wars Story*)

Known to his friends as Chopper, this C1 model astromech droid is a member of General Hera Syndulla's rebel crew. As stubborn as he is mischievous, Chopper begrudgingly goes about his business maintaining Syndulla's ship, the *Ghost*. Chopper is stationed at Yavin 4 in the days leading up to the Battle of Scarif.

R5-D4
(*A New Hope*)

An unremarkable droid by most accounts, the red astromech's brush with R2-D2 and C-3PO makes him noteworthy. Had it not been for a malfunction of the droid's motivator, R5-D4 would have taken R2-D2's place on Luke Skywalker's family farm, forever changing Luke's destiny.

L3-37
(*Solo: A Star Wars Story*)

Lando Calrissian's copilot when he owns the *Millennium Falcon* is the free-thinking droid L3-37. This self-constructed droid connects directly to the ship's navicomputer, making her one of the most advanced navigators in the smuggling business. When her body is destroyed in a firefight on Kessel, Lando uploads her intelligence directly into the *Falcon*'s computer, forever making her part of the ship.

D-O
(*The Rise of Skywalker*)

Primarily used for data storage, D-O is cobbled together from spare parts by an unknown droidsmith. He moves about on a gyroscopic uni-tread wheel and communicates in a simplified form of binary that is easier for non-droids to understand. His long-range antennae assist in the transfer of information.

38

DEADLY DROIDS

THE DEADLIEST DROID WEAPONS AND SOLDIERS

FORGET ETIQUETTE AND PROTOCOL, THESE MECHANICAL MONSTERS SHOW US THAT DROIDS CAN BE DANGEROUS SOLDIERS, DEADLY BOUNTY HUNTERS, OR SECRETIVE SPIES. THEIR LACK OF HUMANITY HELPS THEM BE CALCULATING AND EFFICIENT, AN INDISPENSABLE ADVANTAGE IN THE HEAT OF BATTLE.

B1 BATTLE DROID

(*The Phantom Menace*, *Attack of the Clones*, *Revenge of the Sith*)

The standard battle droid of the Trade Federation and Separatist armies during the Clone Wars, the B1 isn't a sophisticated droid. What they lack in brains they make up for in sheer numbers, relying on a seemingly never-ending supply of droids to overwhelm clones and Jedi in battle. (**Image A**)

DROIDEKA

(*The Phantom Menace*, *Attack of the Clones*, *Revenge of the Sith*)

Their deflector shields and high rate of fire make them a worrying opponent, even to small groups of Jedi. (**Image B**)

DROID STARFIGHTERS

(*The Phantom Menace*, *Attack of the Clones*,
Revenge of the Sith)

The starfighters of the Separatist navy have a major advantage over those of the Republic: They don't require pilots. Just like their infantry counterparts, droid starfighters are stand-alone droids manufactured with built-in intelligence. This often means they significantly outnumber their enemies in battle. (**Image C**)

B2 SUPER BATTLE DROID

(*Attack of the Clones*, *Revenge of the Sith*)

Though they are more costly to produce, the B2 super battle droid is far sturdier than its B1 counterpart. Their mechanical limbs support

integrated weapon systems such as dual wrist blasters. (**Image D**)

11-3K VIPER PROBE DROID
(*Solo: A Star Wars Story*)

Rotating blaster cannons, repulsorlift engines, and capable sensors allow the 11-3K model of probe droid to patrol and police remote areas of Imperial territory. Operating in groups, they can pin down a target and call for backup. (**Image E**)

IG-88
(*The Empire Strikes Back*)

Standing nearly two meters tall and armed with a blaster in each hand, the merciless assassin droid IG-88 serves no master. His mechanical precision allows IG-88 to take shots and move in ways that others cannot. (**Image F**)

4-LOM
(*The Empire Strikes Back*)

The 4-LOM might have the body of a protocol droid, but etiquette is not his primary function. Logic glitches let this droid change his programming and become a bounty hunter, often teaming up with fellow bounty hunter, Zuckuss. (**Image G**)

BB-9E
(*The Last Jedi*)

The First Order's state-of-the art astromech units forego extensive mechanical arms and tooldisks in favor of advanced sensors. This allows them to carefully monitor for abnormal activity including Resistance saboteurs. BB-9E isn't heavily armed but can call upon squads of the *Supremacy*'s First Order stormtroopers in an emergency. (**Image H**)

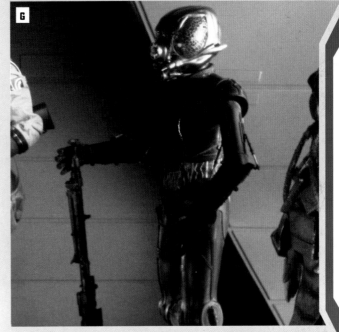

39

NO MATCH FOR A GOOD BLASTER

LIST OF BLASTER TYPES

INELEGANT AS THEY MIGHT BE, BLASTERS ARE THE GALAXY'S MOST COMMON TYPE OF WEAPON. PISTOLS, CARBINES, AND RIFLES ALIKE FIRE ENERGY BLASTS WITH DEVASTATING EFFECTS. FROM HAN SOLO'S GUNSLINGING PISTOL TO THE CHROMED PRECISION OF CAPTAIN PHASMA'S RIFLE, THESE ARE SOME OF THE MOST NOTEWORTHY TYPES OF BLASTERS CARRIED THROUGHOUT THE GALAXY.

HAN SOLO'S DL-44
(*Solo: A Star Wars Story,
A New Hope, The Empire
Strikes Back, Return of the Jedi,
The Force Awakens*)

REY'S LPA NN-14
(*The Force Awakens,
The Last Jedi,
The Rise of Skywalker*)

**CAPTAIN PHASMA'S F-11D
BLASTER RIFLE**
(*The Force Awakens,
The Last Jedi*)

BOBA FETT'S EE-3 CARBINE
(*The Empire Strikes Back,
Return of the Jedi*)

**DIRECTOR KRENNIC'S DT-29
HEAVY BLASTER PISTOL**
(*Rogue One: A Star Wars Story*)

**NABOO S-5 HEAVY BLASTER
PISTOL**
(*The Phantom Menace*)

**LANDO'S SE-14 BLASTER
PISTOL**
(*Solo: A Star Wars Story*)

**TOBIAS BECKETT'S
RSKF-44 HEAVY
BLASTER PISTOL**
(*Solo: A Star Wars Story*)

**JANGO FETT'S WESTAR-34
PISTOLS**
(*Attack of the Clones*)

**CLONE ARMY DC-15
BLASTER RIFLE**
(*Attack of the Clones,
Revenge of the Sith*)

JYN ERSO'S A180 PISTOL
(*Rogue One: A Star Wars Story*)

E-11 BLASTER RIFLE
(*Solo: A Star Wars Story,
Rogue One: A Star Wars Story,
A New Hope, The Empire Strikes Back,
Return of the Jedi*)

QI'RA'S S-195 PISTOL
(*Solo: A Star Wars Story*)

40

JAIL TIME

PRISONS, HOLDING CELLS, LABOR

IN THE ONGOING STRUGGLE BETWEEN GOOD AND EVIL, THE GOOD GUYS SEEM TO SPEND A LOT OF TIME BEHIND BARS. BEING CAPTURED IS JUST ONE OF THE RISKS THEY FACE AND THESE ARE THE PRISONS, HOLDING CELLS, AND LABOR CAMPS WHERE HEROES ARE HELD.

SAW GERRERA'S PARTISAN BASE

(*Rogue One: A Star Wars Story*)

Captured Imperials in Saw Gerrera's holding cells soon learn why this ruthless partisan left them alive: interrogation. After years of struggle against the Empire, Saw doesn't take prisoners because it is the right thing to do. (**Image A**)

DEATH STAR DETENTION BLOCK

(*A New Hope*)

Princess Leia was a temporary resident of cell 2187 on Detention Block AA-23. As the numbers suggest, the giant Death Star battle station has plenty of room for prisoners in multiple detention blocks each holding numerous cells. (**Image B**)

CLOUD CITY

(*The Empire Strikes Back*)

Far below the beautiful, luxurious corridors of Cloud City lies a detention cell. In stark contrast to the bright, open-air quarters elsewhere, this dimly lit cell offers few comforts. After their capture by Darth Vader, heroes Leia, Han, and Chewbacca await their fates here.

JABBA THE HUTT'S DUNGEON
(*Return of the Jedi*)

After years of being in debt to Jabba and on the run, Chewbacca and Han Solo's luck finally runs out. Both are held in the gangster's dungeon until their planned execution by Sarlacc pit.

KYLO REN'S INTERROGATION ROOM
(*The Force Awakens*)

Aboard his Star Destroyer flagship, the *Finalizer*, Kylo Ren has a special interrogation room to pry information out of his captives. The cold, utilitarian room's centerpiece is a single interrogation chair. (**Image C**)

CANTO BIGHT
(*The Last Jedi*)

The casino city of Canto Bight attracts some of the galaxy's most wealthy residents. Where they go, also go thieves, pickpockets, and swindlers looking to take advantage of this gathering of the wealth. When they are caught, the Canto Bight Police hold them in one of the many jail cells in police headquarters. (**Image D**)

GALACTIC GAMES AND ENTERTAINMENT

PASTIMES AROUND THE GALAXY

IN TIMES OF PEACE, CITIZENS OF THE GALAXY FIND TIME TO RELAX AND ENGAGE IN A WIDE VARIETY OF GAMES AND ENTERTAINMENT. FROM SIMPLE CARD AND DICE GAMES TO EXCITING SPORTS SUCH AS PODRACING, THESE PASTIMES PROVIDE A BREAK FROM THE CONSTANT STRUGGLE BETWEEN GOOD AND EVIL.

CHANCE CUBES

(*The Phantom Menace*)

Rolling the dice is a great way to make or settle a bet. Junk trader Watto carries a chance cube wherever he goes. (**Image A**)

PODRACING

(*The Phantom Menace*)

Being illegal doesn't slow down the sport of podracing, whose fans turn out in droves to see their favorite racers fly custom pods at terrifying speeds. Podracers move so quickly that most humans aren't capable of flying one unless they have heightened senses thanks to a connection with the Force.

NUNA-BALL

(*Attack of the Clones*)

This sport is played by two teams of droids but has one organic participant: A tiny nuna creature that serves as the ball. Holograms of the sport play live in the Outlander Club on Coruscant.

GEONOSIAN ARENA EXECUTIONS

(*Attack of the Clones*)

The worker drones of Geonosis find great entertainment watching public executions by exotic beasts in their Petranaki arena.

DEJARIK

(*Solo: A Star Wars Story*, *Rogue One: A Star Wars Story*, *A New Hope*)

Also known as holochess, this board game is popular in secret bases, starships, and residences alike. Though it can be played with physical pieces, the most common version uses holographic pieces. (**Image B**)

SABACC

(*Solo: A Star Wars Story*)

Sabacc is a popular card game played wherever thrillseekers and risk-takers gather. Han Solo wins the *Millennium Falcon* from Lando Calrissian in a game of sabacc on Numidian Prime, having noticed that the scoundrel keeps a card up his sleeve. (**Image C**)

A

B

DROID FIGHTING
(*Solo: A Star Wars Story*)

Though looked down upon by some, droid fighting remains a popular pastime in some of the less sophisticated corners of the galaxy. The droids have no choice but to obey their masters and fight to the death, equipped with various modifications to make the fights more exciting and violent.

SLOT MACHINES
(*The Last Jedi*)

Patrons of the Canto Bight casino fill intricately detailed slot machines with coin after coin in hopes of hitting a jackpot. For these rich visitors, the possibility of winning even more credits is too good to pass by.

FATHIER RACING
(*The Last Jedi*)

Another pastime that draws crowds in Canto Bight, these races involve jockeys atop elegant fathiers bred for speed. The crowds of roaring fans turn a blind eye to the cruel conditions in which the fathiers (and their stable keepers) work.

C

42

FOOD & DRINK

DELICACIES FROM AROUND THE GALAXY

Heroes rarely take the time for a good meal, but even a Jedi must eat occasionally. The most famous dish from *Star Wars* might be blue milk, but it's just one of many delicacies served in a galaxy far, far away.

DEHYDRATED RATIONS
(*The Force Awakens*)

These simple meals of poly-starch and veg-meat provide basic nutrition and last for decades in storage. The junk boss Unkar Plutt uses these rations as a currency, controlling the salvage trade on Jakku by tightly regulating the food supply for the scavengers who toil for him.
(**Image A**)

A

PALLIES

(*The Phantom Menace*)

The pallie is a small, green fruit grown in underground farms and sold by merchants on Tatooine. They are a special treat on the desolate, sandy planet that otherwise doesn't produce much fruit. (**Image B**)

SHURRA FRUIT

(*Attack of the Clones*)

This sweet and delicate fruit is a course during Anakin's and Padmé's dinner on Naboo. The Jedi impresses her with his ability to slice the fruit using a fork, knife, and the Force.

QUANYA RESERVE

(*Solo: A Star Wars Story*)

Dryden Vos's appreciation for the finer things is extended to his guests, whom he serves a quality vintage known as quanya reserve.

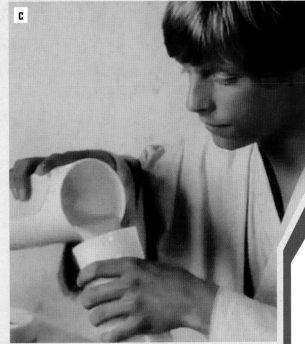

BLUE MILK

(*A New Hope*)

The milk of the bantha, commonly referred to by its unique blue color, is a staple of many diets. Luke Skywalker grew up with blue milk, served by the pitcher by his Aunt Beru on their Tatooine moisture farm. (**Image C**)

SPETAN CHANNELFISH

(*The Last Jedi*)

Another part of Master Skywalker's diet on Ahch-To are fish harvested using a giant spear plunged from the side of a cliff into the depths of the ocean. The reward for this daring maneuver is enough food to sustain him for more than a day.

GREEN MILK

(*The Last Jedi*)

Another variety of animal milk, the green variety comes from the thala-sirens of Ahch-To. As they sun themselves on the rocky shores, Luke Skywalker harvests bottles of the liquid to sustain himself on the isolated planet. (**Image D**)

43

COSMIC COIFFURES

THE OUTLANDISH HAIRDOS AND LUSCIOUS LOCKS OF THE GALAXY

Princess Leia's hair buns from *A New Hope* have become iconic, but they're not the only notable hairstyle in *Star Wars*. Characters throughout the ages sport wild hairdos and luscious locks. In fact, Leia's style is seemingly passed down from her mother, Padmé Amidala, whose wild wardrobes as Queen of the Naboo raised the bar for all hairstyles to follow. Once Padmé steps down as queen and becomes a galactic senator, she still seems to change her hair as often as she changes her clothes.

LIEUTENANT CONNIX
(*The Last Jedi*)

VICE ADMIRAL HOLDO
(*The Last Jedi*)

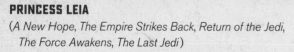

PRINCESS LEIA
(*A New Hope, The Empire Strikes Back, Return of the Jedi, The Force Awakens, The Last Jedi*)

REY
(*The Last Jedi*)

LOVEY
(*The Last Jedi*)

QUEEN AMIDALA
(*The Phantom Menace*)

PADMÉ AMIDALA
(*Attack of the Clones,
Revenge of the Sith*)

44

FINEST FACIAL HAIR

BEARDS, MUSTACHES, AND MORE

HERE ON EARTH, FACIAL HAIR HAS FALLEN INTO, THEN OUT OF, AND NOW BACK INTO STYLE. BUT IN *STAR WARS* STORIES, GREAT FACIAL HAIR HAS ALWAYS BEEN A THING. THE WISE AND NOBLE JEDI OFTEN GROW A BEARD AS THEY AGE. REBEL LEADERS SEEM TO HAVE A PREFERENCE FOR GREAT FACIAL HAIR AS WELL. BUT THEY AREN'T ALONE, AS THESE ARE THE CHARACTERS WITH MUSTACHES, BEARDS, AND MORE.

OBI-WAN KENOBI
(*Attack of the Clones*)

KI-ADI MUNDI
(*The Phantom Menace*)

BARON PAPANOIDA
(*Revenge of the Sith*)

CASSIAN ANDOR
(*Rogue One: A Star Wars Story*)

BIGGS DARKLIGHTER
(*A New Hope*)

CRIX MADINE
(*Return of the Jedi*)

LUKE SKYWALKER
(*The Last Jedi*)

LANDO CALRISSIAN
(*The Empire Strikes Back*)

MASTER CODEBREAKER
(*The Last Jedi*)

DEXTER JETTSTER
(*Attack of the Clones*)

45

CAPED CRUSADERS

CHARACTERS WHO ROCK CAPES AND CLOAKS

In *Solo: A Star Wars Story*, we learn that Lando Calrissian has a longstanding love affair with capes. As a young smuggler, he outfits the *Millennium Falcon* with a closet full of his favorite accessory. As a veteran smuggler, he never loses his sense of style or his charm. While he might wear more of them than anyone else, he's far from the only one to don a space cape.

LANDO CALRISSIAN
(*Rogue One: A Star Wars Story, The Empire Strikes Back, Return of the Jedi, The Rise of Skywalker*)

QI'RA
(*Solo: A Star Wars Story*)

DIRECTOR ORSON KRENNIC
(Rogue One: A Star Wars Story)

BAIL ORGANA
*(Attack of the Clones, Revenge of
the Sith, Rogue One: A Star Wars Story)*

BOBA FETT
*(A New Hope,
The Empire Strikes Back,
Return of the Jedi)*

CAPTAIN PHASMA
(The Force Awakens, The Last Jedi)

DARTH VADER
*(Revenge of the Sith, Rogue One: A Star
Wars Story, A New Hope, The Empire
Strikes Back, Return of the Jedi)*

46

IT'S A DEAL

NEGOTIATIONS AND DEALS MADE FOR PARTS, DROIDS, AND INFORMATION

WHETHER MAKING DEALS FOR STARSHIP PARTS, DROIDS, OR INFORMATION, NEGOTIATING IS AN IMPORTANT SKILL FOR ALL SORTS OF HIGH-STAKES SITUATIONS. FOR SOME OF THESE NEGOTIATORS, THEIR VERY LIFE DEPENDS ON IT.

THE GALACTIC REPUBLIC AND THE TRADE FEDERATION

(*The Phantom Menace*)

The Republic's negotiations with the Trade Federation over Naboo end before they even begin, a consequence of the Trade Federation trying to poison the Jedi negotiators shortly after they arrive.

QUI-GON JINN AND WATTO

(*The Phantom Menace*)

Qui-Gon Jinn gets more than one chance to negotiate with the junk dealer Watto, first for a replacement hyperdrive and later for Anakin Skywalker's freedom. The Jedi is perfectly willing to roll the dice in his negotiation to save the boy, especially when he can use the Force to ensure they roll in his favor. (**Image A**)

BECKETT'S GANG AND DRYDEN VOS

(*Solo: A Star Wars Story*)

When their original plan to steal hyperfuel for crime boss Dryden Vos falls apart, Tobias Beckett negotiates for a second chance. They won't be granted a third.

JAWAS AND UNCLE OWEN

(*A New Hope*)

Looking for a droid to help on a moisture farm on the remote planet of Tatooine leaves Owen Lars few options but to haggle with a band of Jawas dealing in second-hand droids. He doesn't realize that he'll end up paying the ultimate price after purchasing R2-D2 and C-3PO, who are the being pursued by the Empire. (**Image B**)

A

D

BOUSHH AND JABBA THE HUTT

(*Return of the Jedi*)

Leia, disguised as the bounty hunter Boushh, negotiates so well with Jabba the Hutt over Chewbacca's bounty that the Hutt declares her "my kind of scum." (**Image D**)

ROSE TICO AND DJ

(*The Last Jedi*)

DJ demands an upfront payment before he will slice into the First Order's computers. Having little to offer him, Rose begrudgingly agrees to give him her medallion. The piece is not only made of valuable Haysian smelt, it holds deep sentimental value as a reminder of her dearly departed sister.

HAN SOLO AND OBI-WAN KENOBI

(*A New Hope*)

Seeking a pilot to take him to Alderaan, Obi-Wan sits down to negotiate with Han Solo in the Mos Eisley Cantina. The toughest sticking point in the negotiation is Kenobi's need to avoid the Empire, a request that drives up the price substantially. Though the old Jedi can't pay Han's asking price, the smuggler agrees to take partial payment up front along with the promise of even more credits upon arrival.

LANDO CALRISSIAN AND DARTH VADER

(*The Empire Strikes Back*)

Lando makes a deal with the Empire to hand over Luke Skywalker in an attempt to save his city and his friends. Holding all of the power (and an army of stormtroopers), Vader changes the terms of their agreement at will, leaving Calrissian only to pray that he doesn't alter them any further. (**Image C**)

C

B

47

PLAY IT AGAIN, D'AN

THE BEST MUSICIANS/MUSIC GROUPS

MORE OFTEN THAN NOT, GREAT MUSICIANS GO HAND IN HAND WITH PLACES THAT CATER TO ILLEGAL ACTIVITY. THESE TALENTED MUSICIANS OFTEN PLAY IN BARS, CASTLES, AND PLACES OF LUXURY WHERE THE MUSIC STOPS—ONLY BRIEFLY—WHEN SOMEONE LOSES THEIR LIFE. WHILE MOST MIGHT KNOW THE CANTINA BAND SONG, THE MUSICIANS WHO PLAY IT AREN'T YET A HOUSEHOLD NAME. FIGRIN D'AN AND THE MODAL NODES ARE JUST THE HEADLINER FOR THIS LIST OF GALACTIC MUSICIANS.

SHAG KAVA

(*The Force Awakens*)

Maz Kanata's castle plays host to an interesting array of denizens, feeding, housing, and even entertaining them. A band by the name of Shag Kava is in the house when Han Solo visits with Rey and Finn. (**Image A**)

AURODIA VENTAFOLI & LULEO PRIMOC
(*Solo: A Star Wars Story*)

This melodic duo performs for an intimate audience aboard Dryden Vos's yacht. The criminals gathered there appreciate the finer things, including the music. (**Image B**)

FIGRIN D'AN AND THE MODAL NODES
(*A New Hope*)

They just might be the galaxy's most famous musicians. Their hit song, "Mad About Me," is a favorite at the Mos Eisley Cantina. The band's upbeat style brings a little bit of levity to such a rough establishment. The band's leader, Figrin D'an, plays the kloo horn alongside six other Bith musicians. (**Image C**)

MAX REBO BAND
(*Return of the Jedi*)

The band rocking out in Jabba the Hutt's castle isled by Max Rebo playing the red ball jett organ. Eleven musicians accompany him, most notably the singer, Sy Snootles. (**Image D**)

PALANDAG TRIO
(*The Last Jedi*)

A trio of Palandags playing f'nonc horns ensure that the party never stops at the Canto Casino. They're difficult to tell apart, but their names are Dhuz, Hhex, and Jhat. (**Image E**)

48

METHODS OF INTERROGATIONS

KNOWLEDGE IS POWER, AND THESE BADDIES AREN'T AFRAID TO USE THEIR THEIR MIGHT IN THE PURSUIT OF INFORMATION. THE FORCE IS AN EFFECTIVE TOOL WHEN INTERROGATING A PRISONER BUT OTHER METHODS WORK AS WELL. FROM MIND READING TO MIND PROBES, THESE ARE THE MOST EFFECTIVE FORMS OF INTERROGATION.

COUNT DOOKU AND OBI-WAN KENOBI
(*Attack of the Clones*)
Dooku's approach to interviewing Obi-Wan Kenobi is to simply tell him the truth: The Senate is under the control of a Sith Lord. Unfortunately, the truth is so wild that Kenobi can't begin to believe it. (**Image A**)

BOR GULLET AND BODHI ROOK
(*Rogue One: A Star Wars Story*)
Saw Gerrera's partisans use the mind-reading powers of a creature known as Bor Gullet to interrogate the Imperial defector Bodhi Rook. (**Image B**)

DARTH VADER AND LEIA ORGANA
(*A New Hope*)
Vader attempts to use an interrogation droid mind probe to discover the location of the Death Star plans from Princess Leia. Even the Sith Lord is impressed by her resistance to the examination.

DARTH VADER AND HAN SOLO
(*The Empire Strikes Back*)
Vader's interrogation of Han Solo on Cloud City isn't much of an interrogation at all. Instead, Vader is torturing Solo to get the attention of Luke Sky-walker. (**Image C**)

KYLO REN AND POE DAMERON
(*The Force Awakens*)
When the First Order's conventional techniques fail to work on Poe Dameron, Kylo Ren steps in. Ren reaches out through the Force to read Dameron's mind, instantly discovering what others could not. (**Image D**)

49

"YOU MAY FIRE WHEN READY"

THE PLACES DESTROYED OR TARGETED BY A DEATH STAR, A SITH STAR DESTROYER, OR STARKILLER BASE

WHETHER THEY WERE HOUSING REBEL SYMPATHIZERS, THE HOME OF THE NEW REPUBLIC'S DEMOCRACY, OR THE SITE OF A HIDDEN BASE, THESE UNLUCKY PLACES WERE THE TARGET OF THE GALAXY'S ULTIMATE WEAPONS. FALLING UNDER THE CROSSHAIRS OF EITHER DEATH STAR BATTLE STATIONS, THE PLANET-TURNED-SUPERWEAPON STARKILLER BASE, OR A SITH ETERNAL STAR DESTROYER ALMOST ALWAYS LEADS TO DEVASTATING RESULTS, INCLUDING TOTAL DESTRUCTION.

A

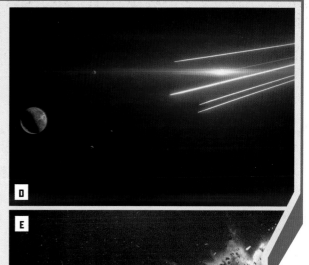

JEOHA/DEATH STAR: PARTIALLY DESTROYED
(*Rogue One: A Star Wars Story*)

THE CITADEL, SCARIF/DEATH STAR: PARTIALLY DESTROYED
(*Rogue One: A Star Wars Story*)
(**Image A**)

ALDERAAN/DEATH STAR: DESTROYED
(*A New Hope*)
(**Image B**)

YAVIN 4/DEATH STAR: TARGETED
(*A New Hope*)

REBEL FLEET, BATTLE OF ENDOR/DEATH STAR II: PARTIALLY DESTROYED
(*Return of the Jedi*)
(**Image C**)

HOSNIAN PRIME/ STARKILLER BASE: DESTROYED
(*The Force Awakens*)
(**Image D**)

D'QAR/STARKILLER BASE: TARGETED
(*The Force Awakens*)

KIJIMI/SITH STAR DESTROYER: DESTROYED
(*The Rise Of Skywalker*)
(**Image E**)

50

FAMOUS HOLOGRAMS

CHARACTERS THAT HAVE APPEARED IN HOLOGRAPHIC FORM

HOLOGRAMS ARE A FORM OF THREE-DIMENSIONAL VIDEO COMMUNICATION FROM A GALAXY FAR, FAR AWAY. WHETHER PART OF A LIVE CONVERSATION OR A RECORDED MESSAGE, THESE ARE THE CHARACTERS WHO FAMOUSLY APPEARED IN HOLOGRAPHIC FORM.

**LEIA ORGANA,
"HELP ME, OBI-WAN KENOBI.
YOU'RE MY ONLY HOPE."**
(*A New Hope, The Last Jedi*)

**DARTH SIDIOUS CALLING
FOR ORDER 66**
(*Revenge of the Sith*)

**OBI-WAN KENOBI TO
THE JEDI COUNCIL**
(*Attack of the Clones*)

LUKE SKYWALKER TO JABBA THE HUTT
(*Return of the Jedi*)

JEDI COUNCIL
(*Revenge of the Sith*)

SUPREME LEADER SNOKE
(*The Force Awakens*)

MAUL
(*Solo: A Star Wars Story*)

GALEN ERSO
(*Rogue One: A Star Wars Story*)

EMPEROR PALPATINE
(*The Empire Strikes Back*)

51

"HOW MANY LANGUAGES DO YOU SPEAK?"

THE MAJOR LANGUAGES OF THE *STAR WARS* GALAXY

JUST AS THE GALAXY IS FILLED WITH DIVERSE PEOPLE AND ALIENS, IT IS ALSO FULL OF UNIQUE LANGUAGES. THOUGH MANY ARE ENTIRELY MADE UP, THESE TONGUES HELP MAKE THE GALAXY FEEL MORE REAL.

A

GALACTIC BASIC

(*The Phantom Menace, Attack of the Clones, Revenge of the Sith, Solo: A Star Wars Story, Rogue One: A Star Wars Story, A New Hope, The Empire Strikes Back, Return of the Jedi, The Force Awakens, The Last Jedi, The Rise of Skywalker*)

The most common language in the galaxy is also the language understood by you and me. Through most of the films, the language you hear is known in the *Star Wars* galaxy as "Galactic Basic."

HUTTESE

(*The Phantom Menace, Attack of the Clones, A New Hope, The Empire Strikes Back, Return of the Jedi, The Force Awakens*)

The crime lords known as the Hutts aren't the only ones who speak their native Huttese. The language is common across the underworld due to their influence. (**Image A**)

B

ASTROMECH BINARY

(*The Phantom Menace*, *Attack of the Clones*, *Revenge of the Sith*, *Solo: A Star Wars Story*, *Rogue One: A Star Wars Story*, *A New Hope*, *The Empire Strikes Back*, *Return of the Jedi*, *The Force Awakens*, *The Last Jedi*, *The Rise of Skywalker*)

Those beeps and boops spoken by astromech droids like R2-D2 are a language known as Astromech Binary. It's similar to other binary languages used by machines and droids, though some people require a translator to understand its meaning.

GUNGANESE

(*The Phantom Menace*)

The native language of the Gungan people is often mixed with words in Galactic Basic, creating a unique hybrid language. When used in context, Gunganese words are generally close enough to Basic to be understood by outsiders.

SHYRIIWOOK

(*Revenge of the Sith*, *Solo: A Star Wars Story*, *A New Hope*, *The Empire Strikes Back*, *Return of the Jedi*, *The Force Awakens*, *The Last Jedi*, *The Rise of Skywalker*)

While many Wookiees understand other languages, they themselves can only speak in their native Shyriiwook, a language of growls and roars.

JAWAESE

(*A New Hope*)

Jawas speak with each other using both verbal language and scent, making it nearly impossible for outsiders to understand them completely.

EWOKESE

(*Return of the Jedi*)

Ewoks speak a strange dialect that even C-3PO finds unfamiliar. (**Image B**)

52

MORE MACHINE THAN MAN

THE CYBORGS OF *STAR WARS*

Whether they enhance natural abilities or replace lost limbs, cybernetics give their owners abilities that they don't possess naturally. Some, like General Grievous, choose to take on these enhancements willingly, while the Decraniated have little choice in the matter. Even animals like the luggabeast have cybernetic enhancements to help them survive in the unforgiving conditions of the planet Jakku.

LOBOT (*The Empire Strikes Back*)

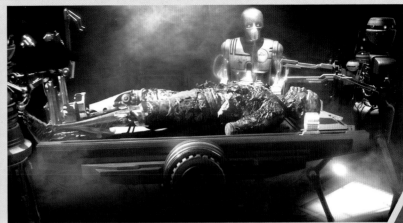

THE DECRANIATED
(*Solo: A Star Wars Story*,
Rogue One: A Star Wars Story)

DARTH VADER (*Revenge of the Sith, A New Hope, The Empire Strikes Back, Return of the Jedi, Rogue One: A Star Wars Story*)

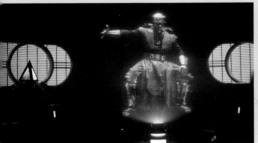

MAUL (*Solo: A Star Wars Story*)

SAW GERRERA (*Rogue One: A Star Wars Story*)

GENERAL GRIEVOUS (*Revenge of the Sith*)

LUGGABEAST
(*The Force Awakens*)

53

NON-CONVENTIONAL WEAPONS

WEAPONS THAT ARE NOT A LIGHTSABER OR BLASTER

SOME CHARACTERS DON'T NEED A BLASTER OR A LIGHTSABER TO DEFEND THEMSELVES. THEY PREFER INVENTIVE OR IMPROVISED WAYS TO APPROACH A FIGHT. THOUGH THERE'S NOTHING CONVENTIONAL ABOUT THESE UNIQUE WEAPONS, THAT DOESN'T MAKE THEM ANY LESS DANGEROUS.

A

B

C

GUNGAN BOOMA
(*The Phantom Menace*)
(**Image A**)

BOBA FETT'S JETPACK
(*The Empire Strikes Back*,
Return of the Jedi) (**Image B**)

KAMINO SABERDART
(*Attack of the Clones*)

GEONOSIAN SONIC BLASTER
(*Attack of the Clones*)
(**Image C**)

ELECTROSTAFF
(*Revenge of the Sith*) (**Image D**)

FORCE PIKE
(*Revenge of the Sith*,
Return of the Jedi)

ELECTRORIPPER STAFF
(*Solo: A Star Wars Story*)
(**Image E**)

TRUNCHEON
(*Rogue One:
A Star Wars Story*)

GAFFI STICK
(*A New Hope*)

THERMAL DETONATOR
(*Return of the Jedi*)

ROSE TICO'S ELECTRO-SHOCK PROD
(*The Last Jedi*) (**Image F**)

JANNAH'S BOW
(*The Rise of Skywalker*)

54

DISTINGUISHED HELMETS

INSTANTLY RECOGNIZABLE HEAD GEAR

These instantly recognizable helmets provide more than just protection for their wearer; they are a show of force. For many, the mere sight of these famous helmets is enough to strike fear into the hearts of their enemies.

JANGO FETT
(Attack of the Clones)

ENFYS NEST
(Solo: A Star Wars Story)

DARTH VADER
(Rogue One: A Star Wars Story, The Force Awakens, A New Hope, The Empire Strikes Back, Return of the Jedi)

IMPERIAL STORMTROOPER
(Solo: A Star Wars Story, Rogue One: A Star Wars Story, A New Hope, The Empire Strikes Back, Return of the Jedi)

LANDO CALRISSIAN'S SKIFF GUARD DISGUISE
(*Return of the Jedi*)

BOUSHH
(*Return of the Jedi*)

KNIGHTS OF REN
(*The Force Awakens, The Rise of Skywalker*)

CAPTAIN PHASMA
(*The Force Awakens, The Last Jedi*)

RED ROYAL GUARD
(*Revenge of the Sith, Return of the Jedi*)

ZORII BLISS
(*The Rise of Skywalker*)

55

LIGHTSABER HILTS

THE LIGHTSABER HILTS OF NOTABLE CHARACTERS

THESE ELEGANT WEAPONS ARE AS DIVERSE AS THE FORCE USERS WHO WIELD THEM. THOUGH THE BASIC CONSTRUCTION OF A LIGHTSABER IS THE SAME, THE HILT STYLE AND MATERIALS VARY WIDELY. CONSIDERING THE ARRAY OF BLADE COLORS PROVIDED BY THE SABERS' KYBER CRYSTALS, IT'S RARE TO FIND TWO LASER SWORDS THAT ARE ALIKE.

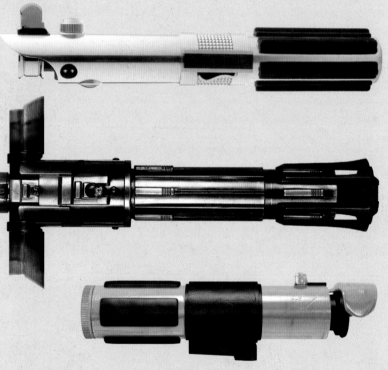

ANAKIN SKYWALKER
(*Revenge of the Sith*)

KYLO REN
(*The Force Awakens,*
The Last Jedi,
The Rise of Skywalker)

YODA
(*Attack of the Clones,*
Revenge of the Sith)

QUI-GON
(*The Phantom Menace*)

COUNT DOOKU

(*Attack of the Clones,*
Revenge of the Sith)

MACE WINDU

(*Attack of the Clones,*
Revenge of the Sith)

OBI-WAN KENOBI

(*Attack of the Clones*)

DARTH MAUL

(*The Phantom Menace*)

DARTH SIDIOUS

(*Revenge of the Sith*)

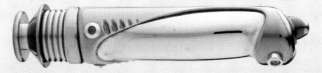

DARTH VADER

(*Rogue One: A Star Wars Story,*
A New Hope, The Empire Strikes
Back, Return of the Jedi)

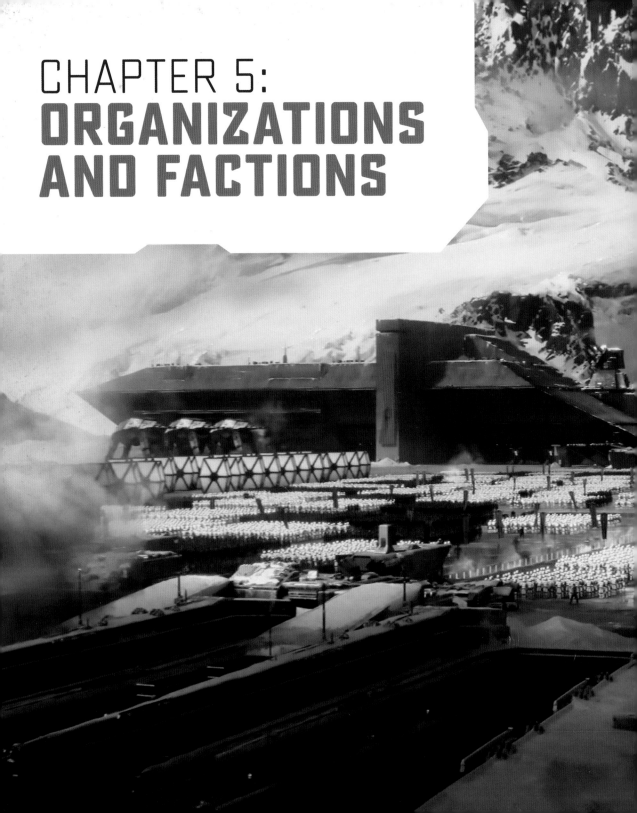

CHAPTER 5:
ORGANIZATIONS AND FACTIONS

56

REBEL ROUSERS

LEADERS AND MILITARY STRATEGISTS OF THE REBELLION AND RESISTANCE

THE REBEL ALLIANCE IS NOTHING WITHOUT ITS BRAVE LEADERS AND MILITARY STRATEGISTS. THE SCRAPPY REBELLION AND RESISTANCE DEPEND ON THE PASSION AND PERSEVERANCE OF THESE LEADERS IN THEIR ONGOING STRUGGLE AGAINST THE FORCES OF EVIL.

MON MOTHMA
(*Rogue One: A Star Wars Story,
Return of the Jedi*)

JAN DODONNA
(*A New Hope, Rogue One: A Star Wars Story*)

BAIL ORGANA
(*Attack of the Clones, Revenge of
the Sith, Rogue One: A Star Wars
Story*)

LEIA ORGANA
(*Rogue One: A Star Wars Story, A New Hope, The
Empire Strikes Back, Return of the Jedi, The Force
Awakens, The Last Jedi, The Rise of Skywalker*)

GENERAL MADINE
(*Return of the Jedi*)

ADMIRAL ACKBAR
(*Return of the Jedi, The Force Awakens, The Last Jedi*)

ADMIRAL RADDUS
(*Rogue One: A Star Wars Story*)

GENERAL RIEEKAN
(*The Empire Strikes Back*)

GENERAL DRAVEN
(*Rogue One: A Star Wars Story*)

SNAP WEXLEY
(*The Force Awakens,
The Rise of Skywalker*)

MAJOR EMATT
(*The Force Awakens,
The Last Jedi*)

VICE ADMIRAL HOLDO
(*The Last Jedi*)

ENFYS NEST
(*Rogue One: A Star Wars
Story*)

SAW GERRERA
(*Rogue One: A
Star Wars Story*)

COMMANDER D'ACY
(*The Last Jedi, The Rise of Skywalker*)

POE DAMERON
(*The Force Awakens, The Last Jedi,
The Rise of Skywalker*)

ADMIRAL STATURA
(*The Force Awakens*)

57

SQUADRONS

REBEL SQUADRON NAMES AND LEADERS

INSPIRED BY FIGHTER GROUPS FROM OUR OWN HISTORY, PILOTS IN *STAR WARS* FORM UP BEHIND BRAVE SQUADRON LEADERS. EACH SQUADRON HAS ITS OWN UNIQUE NAME AND EACH PILOT THEIR CORRESPONDING CALL SIGN. LUKE SKYWALKER WAS PART OF RED SQUADRON AT THE BATTLE OF YAVIN, TAKING THE ROLE OF RED 5 AFTER THE PREVIOUS PILOT PERISHED AT THE BATTLE OF SCARIF. HE LATER TOOK COMMAND OF ROGUE SQUADRON, LEADING IT THROUGH THE BATTLE OF HOTH. BUT LUKE IS JUST ONE OF MANY SQUADRON LEADERS TO SERVE THE REBELLION.

BLUE

(*Rogue One: A Star Wars Story*)

Led by General Antoc Merrick, the X-wings of Blue Squadron are identified by the blue markings that adorn their hulls. This squadron's heavy losses at the Battle of Scarif to secure the Death Star plans precluded it from participating at the Battle of Yavin to destroy the battle station itself. (**Image A**)

RED

(*Rogue One: A Star Wars Story*, *A New Hope*)

Another X-wing squadron that served at the Battle of Scarif, Red Group was also one of two squadrons to see combat against the Death Star. The squadron sustained heavy losses there, including the squadron leader, Garven Dreis, and Luke Skywalker's wingman, Biggs Darklighter. (**Image B**)

GOLD

(*Rogue One: A Star Wars Story*, *A New Hope*)

While Gold Squadron's Y-wing fighter bombers don't excel in dogfights, their exceptional ruggedness and heavy firepower make them ideal of striking hard targets such as capital ships. Members of the squadron, led by Captain "Dutch" Vander, made the initial trench run approach to destroy the Death Star, but were gunned down from behind by Darth Vader and his TIE fighter wingmen. (**Image C**)

GREEN

(*Rogue One: A Star Wars Story,*
Return of the Jedi)

Green Squadron evolved over the course of the
Galactic Civil War, most notably serving as a squadron of A-wings at the Battle of Endor. Its leader
there is Commander Arvel Crynyd, who crashed his
craft into the bridge of the Super Star Destroyer
Executor, a final blow that sent the massive craft
piercing into the second Death Star. (**Image D**)

ROGUE SQUADRON

(*The Empire Strikes Back*)

This squadron is named in honor of the brave crew
of Rogue One and led by Luke Skywalker. The
squadron's most notable test comes at the Battle
of Hoth. There, they work in pilot and gunner teams
to pilot T-47 snowspeeders against Imperial AT-AT
walkers. Wedge Antilles and his gunner Wes Janson
fly as Rogue Three and are the first to use a tow
cable to entangle the Imperial walkers. (**Image E**)

BLUE SQUADRON, THE RESISTANCE

(*The Force Awakens*)

Under the command of Poe Dameron, the Resistance sends Blue Squadron to destroy Starkiller
Base. They carry on a legacy of the Rebel squadrons that came before them while equipped with
updated T-70 X-wing starfighters and RZ-2 model
A-wings. (**Image F**)

CRIMSON & COBALT SQUADRONS, THE RESISTANCE

(*The Last Jedi*)

In addition to their starfighter squadrons, the Resistance fields two squadrons of heavy bombers at
the Battle of D'Qar. Each StarFortress bomber
has a crew of pilots and gunners working together
to deliver the bomber's payload of munitions on
target. The hulking bombers are easy targets for
First Order fighters and Resistance victory comes
at a heavy cost. (**Image G**)

58

KNIGHTS OF NOTE

THE BEST KNOWN JEDI KNIGHTS AND MASTERS

THE JEDI ORDER SERVE AS BOTH SPIRITUAL FOLLOWERS OF THE FORCE AND DEFENDERS OF PEACE FOR THE GALACTIC REPUBLIC. PROSPECTIVE JEDI JOIN THE ORDER AS INFANTS, TRAINING THEIR WHOLE LIVES TO MASTER THE WAYS OF THE FORCE. THESE NOTEWORTHY MEMBERS OF THE ORDER ARE ACTIVE IN THE FINAL YEARS OF THE REPUBLIC, SERVING AT A TIME WHEN THE GOVERNMENT THEY PROTECT IS DESTROYED FROM THE INSIDE BY THEIR RIVALS, THE SITH. THE LEGACY OF THE JEDI EVENTUALLY FALLS TO LUKE SKYWALKER AND REY TO CARRY ON THE TEACHINGS OF THE JEDI.

QUI-GON JINN
(*The Phantom Menace*)

KI-ADI-MUNDI
(*The Phantom Menace, Attack of the Clones, Revenge of the Sith*)

LUMINARA UNDULI
(*Attack of the Clones, Revenge of the Sith*)

MACE WINDU
(*The Phantom Menace, Attack of the Clones, Revenge of the Sith*)

DEPA BILLABA
(*The Phantom Menace, Attack of the Clones*)

AAYLA SECURA
(*Attack of the Clones, Revenge of the Sith*)

PLO KOON
(*The Phantom Menace, Attack of the Clones, Revenge of the Sith*)

ADI GALLIA
(*The Phantom Menace, Attack of the Clones*)

SHAAK TI
(*Attack of the Clones, Revenge of the Sith*)

KIT FISTO
(*Attack of the Clones, Revenge of the Sith*)

OBI-WAN KENOBI
(*The Phantom Menace, Attack of the Clones, Revenge of the Sith, A New Hope, The Empire Strikes Back, Return of the Jedi*)

YODA
(*The Phantom Menace, Attack of the Clones, Revenge of the Sith, The Empire Strikes Back, Return of the Jedi, The Last Jedi*)

ANAKIN SKYWALKER
(*The Phantom Menace, Attack of the Clones, Revenge of the Sith, Return of the Jedi*)

LUKE SKYWALKER
(*A New Hope, The Empire Strikes Back, Return of the Jedi, The Force Awakens, The Last Jedi, The Rise of Skywalker*)

REY
(*The Force Awakens, The Last Jedi, The Rise of Skywalker*)

59

THREATENING TROOPERS

TYPES OF (WHITE CLAD) STORMTROOPERS

Though their origin dates back to the clone troopers of the Galactic Republic, the white armor these troops wear has become synonymous with the Galactic Empire. Decades after the Empire's fall, the First Order fields modernized troopers for its armies as they seek to regain the absolute power that its predecessor lost. Both armies employ a wide array of trooper types, from the standard stormtrooper armor to specialized variants designed to deal with specific battlefield challenges.

FIRST ORDER

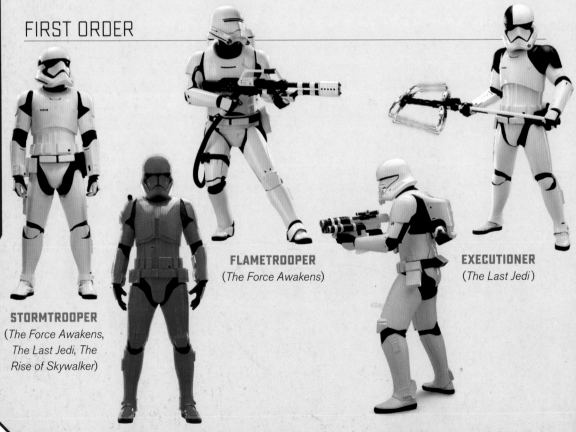

FLAMETROOPER
(*The Force Awakens*)

EXECUTIONER
(*The Last Jedi*)

STORMTROOPER
(*The Force Awakens, The Last Jedi, The Rise of Skywalker*)

SITH STORMTROOPER
(*The Rise of Skywalker*)

JET TROOPER
(*The Rise of Skywalker*)

IMPERIAL

STORMTROOPER

(*Solo: A Star Wars Story, Rogue One: A Star Wars Story, A New Hope, The Empire Strikes Back, Return of the Jedi*)

PATROL TROOPER

(*Solo: A Star Wars Story*)

RANGE TROOPER

(*Solo: A Star Wars Story*)

DEATH TROOPER

(*Rogue One: A Star Wars Story*)

MUDTROOPER

(*Solo: A Star Wars Story*)

SNOWTROOPER

(*The Empire Strikes Back*)

SCOUT TROOPER

(*Return of the Jedi*)

SHORETROOPER

(*Rogue One: A Star Wars Story*)

60

SERVANTS OF THE EMPIRE

CENTRAL FIGURES OF THE IMPERIAL MILITARY AND LEADERSHIP

THEY'RE CALCULATING, SHARPLY DRESSED, AND MOST HAVE BRITISH ACCENTS: THEY'RE THE LOYAL SERVANTS OF THE EMPIRE. WHILE THEY'VE ALL SWORN ALLEGIANCE TO THE EMPEROR, THEIR SECOND LOYALTY LIES TO THEMSELVES AS THEY JOCKEY FOR POWER AND INFLUENCE INSIDE THE IMPERIAL MILITARY MACHINE. IT'S A DANGEROUS GAME TO PLAY. AFTER ALL, LOSING THE GAME MEANS LOSING YOUR LIFE.

GRAND MOFF TARKIN
(*Revenge of the Sith*, *Rogue One: A Star Wars Story*, *A New Hope*)

DIRECTOR KRENNIC
(*Rogue One: A Star Wars Story*)

GENERAL TAGGE
(*A New Hope*)

ADMIRAL MOTTI
(*A New Hope*)

ADMIRAL OZZEL
(*The Empire Strikes Back*)

CAPTAIN NEEDA
(*The Empire Strikes Back*)

GENERAL VEERS
(*The Empire Strikes Back*)

ADMIRAL PIETT
(*The Empire Strikes Back, Return of the Jedi*)

MOFF JERJERROD
(*Return of the Jedi*)

61

FIRST THINGS FIRST

THE FIRST ORDER'S LEADERS AND KEY MEMBERS

From the spy Bazine Netal to the veteran Captain Canady, these leaders and members of the First Order are staunch supporters of their organization's vision to bring order to a chaotic galaxy. Armed with the finest in military training and equipment, they will go to any length to see the New Republic and the Resistance destroyed.

CAPTAIN PHASMA
(*The Force Awakens, The Last Jedi*)

COLONEL DATOO

(The Force Awakens)

GENERAL HUX

(The Force Awakens, The Last Jedi, The Rise of Skywalker)

BAZINE NETAL

(The Force Awakens)

CAPTAIN OPAN

(The Last Jedi)

CAPTAIN OPAN

(The Last Jedi)

ALLEGIANT GENERAL PRYDE

(The Rise of Skywalker)

62

BOUNTY HUNTERS NOT NAMED FETT

FAMOUS GUNS FOR HIRE

THE GREATEST COLLECTION OF BOUNTY HUNTERS IS FOUND ON THE BRIDGE OF DARTH VADER'S STAR DESTROYER IN *THE EMPIRE STRIKES BACK*. THE HUNTERS ASSEMBLED TO TRACK DOWN HAN SOLO AND THE *MILLENNIUM FALCON* ARE SOME OF THE MOST RENOWNED TO EVER TAKE UP THE MANTLE. WHILE BOBA FETT MIGHT BE THE MOST FAMOUS BOUNTY HUNTER IN THE GALAXY, THESE ARE HIS NOTEWORTHY CONTEMPORARIES.

AURRA SING
(*The Phantom Menace, Solo: A Star Wars Story*)

This background bounty hunter makes a brief appearance in *The Phantom Menace* as a podracing spectator. Nearly twenty years later, she is mentioned again in *Solo: A Star Wars Story* when Tobias Beckett reveals he infamously pushed Sing to her death. (**Image A**)

ZAM WESELL
(*Attack of the Clones*)

Wesell is a member of the Clawdite species, giving her the ability to shapeshift to look like others. It's the perfect ability for a bounty hunter and assassin who needs to blend into a crowd. (**Image B**)

GREEDO
(*A New Hope*)

Greedo's last job is tracking Han Solo for Jabba the Hutt. The careless hunter underestimates Solo, a mistake that costs him his life in the Mos Eisley Cantina. (**Image C**)

DENGAR
(*The Empire Strikes Back*)

Dengar is heavily armored and heavily scarred, all evidence of a rough life tracking bounties during the Clone Wars and later the Galactic Civil War. (**Image D**)

IG-88
(The Empire Strikes Back)

This assassin droid has no owner, instead taking on bounties to make a living as a free droid. (**ImageE**)

BOSSK
(The Empire Strikes Back)

Perhaps no one looks more like a predator than Bossk. The reptilian Trandoshan is particularly notorious as a hunter of Wookiees, a popular pursuit among others of his species. (**Image F**)

4-LOM
(The Empire Strikes Back)

A frequent partner of Zuckuss, 4-LOM has the body of a protocol droid but the programming of a killer. As a droid, he can calculate and anticipate the moves of his targets. (**Image G**)

ZUCKUSS
(The Empire Strikes Back)

Zuckuss wears a mask that allows him to breathe ammonia instead of oxygen. Like others of his species, the Gand earned a reputation for his tracking skills. (**Image H**)

63

HONOR THE FALLEN

THE MANY BRAVE REBEL AND RESISTANCE FIGURES WHO GAVE THEIR LIVES FOR THEIR CAUSE

To turn the tide in the lopsided struggle between the outnumbered and outgunned Rebellion and Resistance, these brave freedom fighters gave their lives for the good of their cause. Without their sacrifices, evil would reign over the whole of the galaxy. These are the many brave figures we lost in the fight for peace and justice.

SAW GERRERA
(*Rogue One: A Star Wars Story*)

ADMIRAL RADDUS
(*Rogue One: A Star Wars Story*)

CASSIAN ANDOR
(*Rogue One: A Star Wars Story*)

JYN ERSO
(*Rogue One: A Star Wars Story*)

BAZE MALBUS
(*Rogue One: A Star Wars Story*)

BODHI ROOK
(*Rogue One: A Star Wars Story*)

K-2SO
(*Rogue One: A Star Wars Story*)

CHIRRUT ÎMWE
(Rogue One: A Star Wars Story)

JEK PORKINS
(A New Hope)

BIGGS DARKLIGHTER
(A New Hope)

DAK RALTER
(The Empire Strikes Back)

ELLO ASTY
(The Force Awakens)

PAIGE TICO
(The Last Jedi)

TALLISSAN "TALLIE" LINTRA
(The Last Jedi)

ADMIRAL ACKBAR
(The Last Jedi)

VICE ADMIRAL HOLDO
(The Last Jedi)

64

POLITICAL PROWESS

POWERFUL MOVERS AND SHAKERS

MILITARY LEADERS AREN'T THE ONLY FIGURES OF AUTHORITY IN THE GALAXY. THESE SENATORS, CHIEFTAINS, AND LEADERS PLAY AN ESSENTIAL ROLE ON THEIR SCATTERED WORLDS. WHETHER DEMOCRATIC CHANCELLORS OR LEADERS OF THE SEPARATIST ALLIANCE, THESE AUTHORITIES HOLD THE FATE OF THEIR PEOPLE—AND SOMETIMES THE GALAXY—IN THEIR HANDS.

CHANCELLOR VALORUM
(*The Phantom Menace*)

Chancellor, Galactic Republic

MAS AMEDDA
(*The Phantom Menace, Attack of the Clones, Revenge of the Sith*)

Vice Chair, Galactic Senate (**Image A**)

BOSS NASS
(*The Phantom Menace, Revenge of the Sith*)

Boss of the Gungans

ORN FREE TA
(*The Phantom Menace, Attack of the Clones, Revenge of the Sith*)

Senator of Ryloth, Galactic Republic (**Image B**)

NUTE GUNRAY
(*The Phantom Menace, Attack of the Clones, Revenge of the Sith*)

Viceroy, Trade Federation (**Image C**)

LAMA SU
(*Attack of the Clones*)

Prime Minister, Kamino

POGGLE THE LESSER
(*Attack of the Clones, Revenge of the Sith*)

Archduke of Geonosis

SAN HILL
(*Attack of the Clones, Revenge of the Sith*)

Chairman, Intergalactic Banking Clan

TION MEDON
(*Revenge of the Sith*)

Port Administrator, Utapau (**Image D**)

CHIEF CHIRPA
(*Return of the Jedi*)

Chief, Bright Tree Village

CHANCELLOR VILLECHAM
(*The Force Awakens*)

Chancellor, New Republic

A

B

C

D

65

GALACTIC SMARTIES

THE SMARTEST SCIENTISTS, SCHOLARS, AND RELIGIOUS FIGURES IN THE GALAXY

THESE SCIENTISTS, SCHOLARS, AND RELIGIOUS FIGURES APPLY THEIR CONSIDERABLE EXPERTISE TO THEIR CHOSEN FIELDS, BRINGING WISDOM AND GRACE IN TIMES OF UNCERTAINTY. THEY PROVIDE A SOPHISTICATED CONTRAST TO A GALAXY TEEMING WITH SOLDIERS, SCOUNDRELS, AND BRUTES.

GALEN ERSO
(*Rogue One: A Star Wars Story*)

While he always intended to use his research for the greater good, the genius of Galen Erso is pressed into service for the Galactic Empire. Though he plays a role in the Death Star's development, he also manages to outsmart his Imperial masters and design a fault into the superweapon. (**Image A**)

JOCASTA NU
(*Attack of the Clones*)

Jocasta Nu is both Jedi Master and Chief Librarian of the Jedi archives. She oversees one of the most impressive collections of knowledge known in the galaxy, including its substantial vaults of ancient holocrons and relics. (**Image B**)

SIO BIBBLE
(*The Phantom Menace, Revenge of the Sith*)

Bibble serves as a trusted advisor to Queen Amidala during the trade crisis on Naboo. The experienced politician rightly predicts the Trade Federation invasion. (**Image C**)

D

E

F

LOR SAN TEKKA
(*The Force Awakens*)

Though he cannot manipulate the Force himself, this explorer is also a spiritual follower of the Church of the Force. He plays a critical role helping the Resistance find Luke Skywalker and bravely stands up to Kylo Ren in his final moments. (**Image D**)

DEXTER JETTSTER
(*Attack of the Clones*)

When Obi-Wan Kenobi has a question even the Jedi archives can't answer, he turns to his trusted friend, Dex. This unassuming owner of a diner has years of experience prospecting in the furthest reaches of the galaxy, gaining experience and knowledge unrivaled by most. (**Image E**)

LOGRAY
(*Return of the Jedi*)

Logray is a trusted advisor to Chief Chirpa and the Chief Shaman of his Ewok tribe. (**Image F**)

JABBA'S PAYROLL

THE ALIEN STAFF, BOUNTY HUNTERS, AND LOWLIFES WHO WORK FOR JABBA THE HUTT

Notorious gangster Jabba the Hutt always plays host to a full palace. He surrounds himself with staff, bounty hunters, and lowlifes to do his dirty work or simply provide entertainment. Though Ephant Mon is a trusted friend, Jabba treats many of these beings with contempt. Most are attracted to Jabba purely for his power or money, just as he cares only for the function they provide.

A

BIB FORTUNA
(*The Phantom Menace*, *Return of the Jedi*)
(**Image A**)

GREEDO
(*A New Hope*)

EV-9D9
(*Return of the Jedi*) (**Image B**)

SALACIOUS B. CRUMB
(*Return of the Jedi*) (**Image C**)

EPHANT MON
(*Return of the Jedi*) (**Image D**)

BOBA FETT
(*Return of the Jedi*)

J'QUILLE
(*Return of the Jedi*)

MALAKILI
(*Return of the Jedi*)

REE-YEES
(*Return of the Jedi*)

TESSEK
(*Return of the Jedi*)

MAX REBO'S BAND
(*Return of the Jedi*)

D

B

C

67

GANGS AND GANGSTERS

OUTLAW GROUPS AND THEIR LEADERS

Outlaws of all stripes operate on the fringes of galactic society. While the war for control of the galaxy rages, they seek to build their own criminal empires in the underworld. From small time gangs to sprawling syndicates, these are the galaxy's most notorious outlaw groups.

A

B

THE HUTTS
(*The Phantom Menace*, *A New Hope*, *Return of the Jedi*)

Jabba the Hutt is just one of the Hutt crime lords that rule in parts of the Outer Rim. For some lawless places, the Hutts are the closest thing they have to a government, overseeing trade and disputes in the territory under their control.

THE PYKE SYNDICATE
(*Solo: A Star Wars Story*)

The secretive Pykes primarily trade in illegal spice, a substance of great value on the black market. Their crimes also extend to the slave trade that provides manual labor for the spice mines they oversee. Pyke operations span from Mandalore to Kessel, and many points in between. (**Image A**)

ENFYS NEST'S MARAUDERS
(*Solo: A Star Wars Story*)

Enfys Nest builds a band of marauders from war-torn planets across the galaxy. They work in tandem to steal valuable goods atop their high-flying swoop bikes, earning them the name Cloud-Riders. Though some see them as pirates, others understand that they are rebels fighting for the greater good.

GUAVIAN DEATH GANG
(*The Force Awakens*)

Unscrupulous loans are just part of the Guavian Death Gang's criminal enterprise. They collect on debts by employing cybernetically enhanced soldiers, each equipped with black market weapons and technology. (**Image B**)

CRIMSON DAWN
(*Solo: A Star Wars Story*)

Publicly, the Crimson Dawn criminal organization follows the command of Dryden Vos but a far more sinister leader rules from the shadows. The former Sith apprentice, Maul, commands this far-reaching syndicate with the goal of amassing enough underworld power to take revenge on those who wronged him. After Vos's death, Maul appoints Qi'ra to lead the operation.

WHITE WORMS
(*Solo: A Star Wars Story*)

Operating from the underworld of Corellia, the White Worms run a black market operation using a network of child scavengers. These scrumrats serve at the pleasure of the White Worm leader, Lady Proxima.

KANJIKLUB
(*The Force Awakens*)

The Kanjiklub were once themselves slaves to the Hutts, but upon gaining their freedom took up their own criminal enterprise. Their leader, Tasu Leech, made the mistake of loaning money to the smuggler Han Solo, not realizing that the old scoundrel was already in over his head. (**Image C**)

ZORII BLISS & THE SPICE RUNNERS OF KIJIMI
(*The Rise of Skywalker*)

Zorii and her band of underworld hooligans filled the void left in the spice trade, after the collapse of the Empire and the death of Jabba the Hutt. The group specialized in all manner of criminal activities, from the sale of spice and forgery to piracy and protection. Essentially, pay or be plundered.

C

68

"TO ME SHE'S ROYALTY"

THE QUEENS AND PRINCESSES

WHILE PRINCESS LEIA MIGHT BE THE MOST FAMOUS NOBLE IN A GALAXY FAR, FAR AWAY, THE PLANET NABOO GIVES US MOST OF THE ROYALTY ON THIS LIST. ON NABOO, THE MONARCHY IS NOT INHERITED BUT INSTEAD ELECTED BY THE PEOPLE TO SERVE SHORT TERMS AS KING OR QUEEN.

QUEEN AMIDALA

(*The Phantom Menace*)

After the Naboo crisis is over, she steps down from her role as queen and becomes Naboo's Senate representative.

QUEEN JAMILLIA
(*Attack of the Clones*)

Queen Jamillia serves as Naboo's queen at the outbreak of the Clone Wars. Like other Naboo queens, she is elected to the post for a short reign. (**Image A**)

QUEEN APAILANA
(*Revenge of the Sith*)

Queen Apailana is just twelve years old when elected Queen of the Naboo. She is the ruling monarch at the end of the Clone Wars, overseeing the former Queen Amidala's funeral. (**Image B**)

QUEEN BREHA ORGANA
(*Revenge of the Sith*)

Queen Breha is the last ruling monarch of her planet, reigning as queen at the time of Alderaan's destruction at the hands of the Empire. (**Image C**)

PRINCESS LEIA ORGANA
(*Rogue One: A Star Wars Story*, *A New Hope*, *The Empire Strikes Back*, *Return of the Jedi*, *The Force Awakens*, *The Last Jedi*, *The Rise of Skywalker*)

Leia Organa takes many titles through the course of her life, but her first is Princess of Alderaan. (**Image D**)

69

WARRIORS

THE GREATEST WARRIOR CULTURES IN THE GALAXY

IN A GALAXY THAT'S CONSTANTLY FIGHTING, THESE WARRIOR CULTURES HAVE A DEFINITE ADVANTAGE. THESE GROUPS EXCEL IN BATTLE, WHETHER FROM YEARS OF EXPERIENCE OR THANKS TO BIOLOGICAL ADVANTAGES ENJOYED BY THEIR SPECIES. SOME, SUCH AS THE EWOKS OR GUNGANS, MIGHT BE A SURPRISING ADDITION, BUT THEY HAVE MORE THAN PROVED THEIR VALUE AS WARRIORS WHEN IT MATTERED MOST.

A

GUNGANS
(*The Phantom Menace*)

TUSKEN RAIDERS
(*The Phantom Menace, A New Hope*)

WEEQUAY
(*The Phantom Menace, Attack of the Clones, Revenge of the Sith, Return of the Jedi*)

WOOKIEES
(*The Phantom Menace, Revenge of the Sith, Solo: A Star Wars Story, A New Hope, The Empire Strikes Back, Return of the Jedi, The Force Awakens, The Last Jedi, The Rise of Skywalker*)

GEONOSIANS
(*Revenge of the Sith*)

CLOUD-RIDERS
(*Solo: A Star Wars Story*) (**Image A**)

MIMBANESE
(*Solo: A Star Wars Story*) (**Image B**)

EWOKS
(*Return of the Jedi*)

KNIGHTS OF REN
(*The Force Awakens, The Rise of Skywalker*) (**Image C**)

JANNAH'S TRIBE
(*The Rise of Skywalker*)

70

ON GUARD

BODYGUARDS AND SECURITY FORCES

KEEPING THE PEACE IS NO SMALL TASK WHEN EVERYONE IS CONSTANTLY AT WAR. SECURITY FALLS TO THESE BODYGUARDS, POLICE, AND SECURITY FORCES TO PROTECT THE POPULATION OR HIGH-PROFILE INDIVIDUALS.

GALACTIC SENATE GUARD
(*The Phantom Menace*)

NABOO PALACE GUARD
(*The Phantom Menace*)

REBEL ALLIANCE HONOR GUARDS
(*A New Hope*) **(Image A)**

CLOUD CITY WING GUARD
(*The Empire Strikes Back*)

JABBA THE HUTT'S GAMORREAN GUARDS
(*Return of the Jedi*)

IMPERIAL ROYAL GUARDS
(*Return of the Jedi*)

DRYDEN VOS'S HYLOBON GUARDS
(*Solo: A Star Wars Story*) **(Image B)**

ELITE PRAETORIAN GUARD
(*The Last Jedi*) **(Image C)**

CANTO BIGHT POLICE
(*The Last Jedi*)

KNIGHTS OF REN
(*The Force Awakens, The Rise of Skywalker*) **(Image D)**

C

B

A

CHAPTER 6:
GALACTIC EVENTS

71

MAJOR SPACE BATTLES

BIGGEST BATTLES IN STARSHIPS

IT JUST WOULDN'T BE *STAR WARS* WITHOUT A SPACE BATTLE. THAT IS, UNLESS IT'S *THE EMPIRE STRIKES BACK*. OTHERWISE, SPACE BATTLES ARE A DEFINING ELEMENT OF *STAR WARS* FILMS, WHICH LIVES UP TO ITS NAME BY DELIVERING EPIC BATTLES AMONG THE STARS. THESE ARE THE BIGGEST SPACE CONFRONTATIONS THE FILMS HAVE TO OFFER.

TRADE FEDERATION CONTROL SHIP
(*The Phantom Menace*)

The Trade Federation's blockade of Naboo hinges on their ability to control their droids from a central control ship in space. An unlikely hero piloting a starfighter, a 9-year-old Anakin Skywalker, manages to destroy the control ship from the inside. His feat deactivates the droid army on the ground and secures victory for the Gungans and Naboo.

CORUSCANT
(*Revenge of the Sith*)

Near the end of the Clone Wars, the Separatists launch an assault on the Republic's capital planet,

Coruscant. They aim to kidnap the Republic Chancellor, but are foiled by the Clone Navy and Jedi Order. (**Image A**)

SCARIF SHIELD GATE
(*Rogue One: A Star Wars Story*)

The entire planet of Scarif is encased in a giant energy shield, with the shield gate providing the

only way in or out. The rebel fleet, led by Admiral Raddus, clash with Imperial defenders to destroy the gate and allow the ground team to complete their mission to steal the Death Star plans. (**Image B**)

DEATH STAR
(*A New Hope*)

At the Battle of Yavin, the fate of the Rebel Alliance rests in the hands of two squadrons of fighter pilots. They use their small size and maneuverability to avoid the Death Star's defenses, lining up a torpedo attack on a thermal exhaust port to set off a chain reaction that will destroy the moon-sized battle station.

DEATH STAR II
(*Return of the Jedi*)

At the Battle of Endor, the bulk of the Alliance fleet mounts a full assault on the second Death Star.

While the opposing capital ships engage on the perimeter, Lando Calrissian and Wedge Antilles fly into the belly of beast to strike the battle station's power core. (**Image C**)

STARKILLER BASE
(*The Force Awakens*)

The X-wings of Blue Squadron attack the planet-sized superweapon's thermal oscillator in concert with a strike team on the ground.

D'QAR
(*The Last Jedi*)

As the Resistance tries to evacuate their base, the First Order fleet arrives to extract revenge. Pilot Poe Dameron leads the defense as the fleet escapes, managing to take down a First Order Dreadnought in the process but at a heavy cost of life.

72

BIGGEST GROUND BATTLES

MAJOR PLANETARY BATTLES

Don't let the name of the franchise fool you, not all *Star Wars* battles happen in the stars. These are the major planetary battles that decided the fate of the galaxy.

GREAT GRASS PLAINS BATTLE
(*The Phantom Menace*)

The Gungan Grand Army engages in a diversionary attack on the Trade Federation's droid army, allowing the Naboo to retake their capital. (**Image A**)

GEONOSIS
(*Attack of the Clones*)

Upon discovering a droid army being manufactured on Geonosis and the Confederacy's plans to break from the Republic, the Grand Army of clones strikes first to begin the Clone Wars.

UTAPAU
(*Revenge of the Sith*)

The Separatists council takes refuge on Utapau but is discovered by the Republic.

KASHYYYK
(*Revenge of the Sith*)

Clones, Jedi, and Wookiees work together to defend the Wookiee home world from Separatist invasion.

MIMBAN
(*Solo: A Star Wars Story*)

A drawn-out war in the muddy trenches of Mimban pits Imperial conquerors against the natives trying to defend their home. (**Image B**)

SCARIF
(*Rogue One: A Star Wars Story*)

Rebels, led by Rogue One, mount an assault on the Imperial Citadel Tower to steal the Death Star plans.

HOTH
(*The Empire Strikes Back*)

Imperial walkers lead the assault against the Echo Base as the rebels attempt to evacuate before time runs out. (**Image C**)

ENDOR
(*Return of the Jedi*)

Han Solo leads a strike team to destroy the ground-based shield generator protecting the second Death Star.

TAKODANA
(*The Force Awakens*)

First Order spies attract Kylo Ren and his stormtroopers to Maz Kanata's castle in search of BB-8. The Resistance arrives just in time to fight back against the assault.

C

STARKILLER BASE
(*The Force Awakens*)

Han Solo once again leads a team to infiltrate the defenses of a super weapon. This time, he leads Chewbacca and Finn to detonate explosives that reveal the station's weak point to air assault.

CRAIT
(*The Last Jedi*)

Cornered in an abandoned rebel base, General Leia and the Resistance prepare to make a final stand against the First Order. (**Image D**)

D

73

EPIC LIGHTSABER DUELS

SPECTACULAR SHOWDOWNS WITH *STAR WARS'* ICONIC WEAPON

LIGHTSABER DUELS ARE MORE THAN JUST A FIGHT BETWEEN TWO CHARACTERS. THEY ARE THE CULMINATION OF CHARACTER ARCS, A TEST FOR HEROES AND VILLAINS ALIKE, AND A CLIMACTIC CLASH BETWEEN GOOD AND EVIL. WHETHER THEY GIVE US UNLIKELY ALLIES OR LONG-ANTICIPATED REMATCHES, YOU CAN ALMOST ALWAYS COUNT ON A STUNNING ENDING.

DARTH MAUL VS. QUI-GON JINN
(*The Phantom Menace*) (**Image A**)

DARTH MAUL VS. QUI-GON JINN AND OBI-WAN KENOBI
(*The Phantom Menace*)

COUNT DOOKU VS. YODA
(*Attack of the Clones*)

ANAKIN SKYWALKER AND OBI-WAN KENOBI VS. COUNT DOOKU
(*Attack of the Clones*)

ANAKIN SKYWALKER AND OBI-WAN KENOBI VS. COUNT DOOKU
(*Revenge of the Sith*) (**Image B**)

DARTH SIDIOUS VS. MACE WINDU
(*Revenge of the Sith*) (**Image C**)

YODA VS. DARTH SIDIOUS
(*Revenge of the Sith*)

ANAKIN SKYWALKER VS. OBI-WAN KENOBI
(*Revenge of the Sith*) (**Image D**)

DARTH VADER VS. OBI-WAN KENOBI
(*A New Hope*)

LUKE SKYWALKER VS. DARTH VADER
(*The Empire Strikes Back*)

LUKE SKYWALKER VS. DARTH VADER
(*Return of the Jedi*) (**Image E**)

FINN VS. KYLO REN
(*The Force Awakens*)

REY VS. KYLO REN
(*The Force Awakens*)

KYLO REN AND REY VS. PRAETORIAN GUARDS
(*The Last Jedi*) (**Image F**)

REY VS. KYLO REN
(*The Rise of Skywalker*)

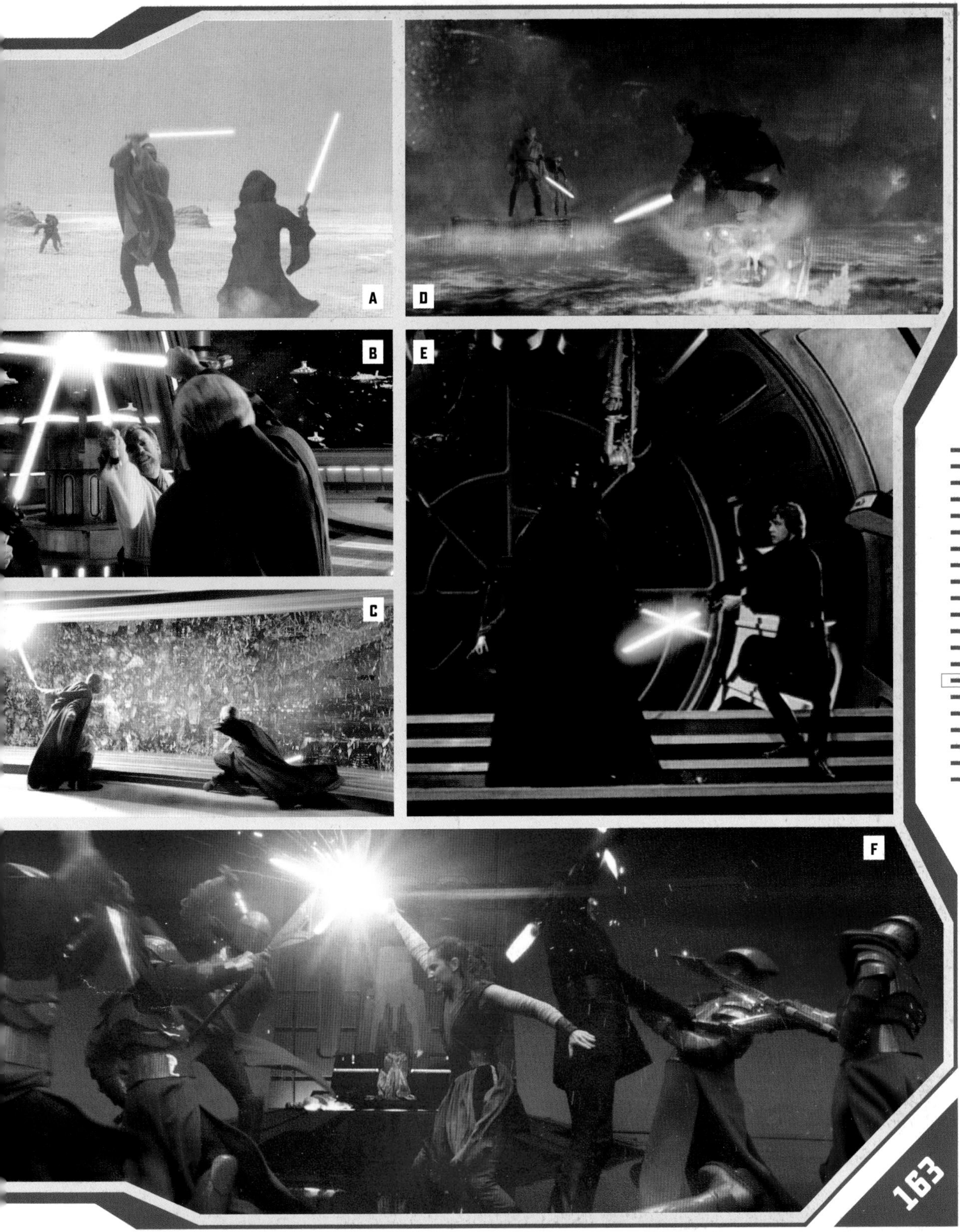
A
D
B
E
C
F

74

OUTSMARTING THE ENEMY

A FEW INSTANCES WHEN A REBEL, BOUNTY HUNTER, ETC. OUTSMARTED THE EMPIRE

AGAINST ALL ODDS, OUTGUNNED REBELS AND SCRAPPY SCOUNDRELS MUST FIND A WAY TO DEFEAT THEIR BETTER EQUIPPED, MORE POWERFUL FOES. THEY OFTEN RELY ON THEIR ABILITY TO OUTSMART THEIR ENEMY, CLEVERLY TURNING THE ODDS IN THEIR FAVOR TO WIN THE DAY. THESE ARE THOSE INSTANCES WHERE REBEL AND SCOUNDREL INGENUITY OUTSMARTED THE EMPIRE.

ROGUE ONE INFILTRATING SCARIF
(*Rogue One: A Star Wars Story*)

Thanks to the former Imperial pilot, Bodhi Rook, and a stolen Imperial shuttle, a whole strike team of Rebels manage to sneak into one of the most heavily guarded installations in the galaxy.

GALEN ERSO'S SABOTAGE OF THE DEATH STAR
(*Rogue One: A Star Wars Story*)

Though the Empire uses Erso's genius to perfect the Death Star's laser weapon, he also designs a fatal flaw into the space station that will lead to its destruction.

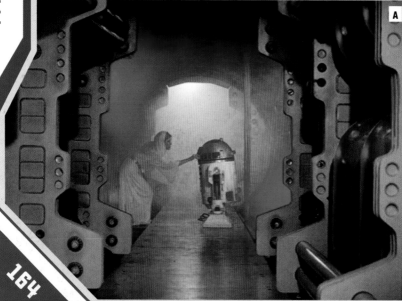

A

PRINCESS LEIA'S MISSION FOR R2-D2
(*A New Hope*)

The Death Star plans slip through the Empire's grasp thanks to some quick thinking by Princess Leia. She gives the plan to R2-D2, who the Imperials mistakenly disregard. (**Image A**)

STORMTROOPER DISGUISE
(*A New Hope*)

Using stolen stormtrooper armor, Han and Luke manage to sneak into the Death Star detention block to rescue Princess Leia.

TRIPPING AT-ATS
(*The Empire Strikes Back*)
While the rebels lack weapons to counter the armor of a hulking AT-AT walker, they cleverly use tow cables to trip the armored vehicle's legs. (**Image B**)

HAN SOLO'S AT-ST RUSE
(*Return of the Jedi*)

Han Solo tricks the Imperial garrison on Endor into opening the doors of their bunker by commandeering an AT-ST and pretending to be its pilot.

HAN SOLO AND CHEWBACCA'S ESCAPE
(*Solo: A Star Wars Story*)

Han and Chewbacca stage a fight on Mimban to distract their Imperial guards from their true objective: Breaking out of jail. (**Image C**)

BECKETT'S TRAIN HEIST
(*Solo: A Star Wars Story*)

Beckett formulates a complex plan to steal coaxium hyperfuel from an Imperial transport. Using explosives and a stolen Imperial hauler, he aims to lift the entire train car full of the valuable substance.

C

75

RESCUE ME

THE TIGHT SPOTS HEROES NEEDED RESCUING FROM

When a mission doesn't go exactly as planned, the situation often calls for a rescue. Based on the number of rescues here, it's clear things rarely go as intended. These are the tight spots from which characters needed rescuing.

ANAKIN SKYWALKER SAVING JAR JAR BINKS FROM SEBULBA

(*The Phantom Menace*)

Jar Jar's clumsiness lands him in trouble with the angriest podracing pilot around, Sebulba. Thanks to the quick thinking of a 9-year-old, Jar Jar gets away with his life.

GEONOSIS ARENA

(*Attack of the Clones*)

Anakin and Padmé's rescue attempt of Obi-Wan backfires, leading to all three being prisoners of the Geonosians. They narrowly avoid execution thanks to the arrival of the Jedi Order and the newly acquired clone army. **(Image A)**

CHANCELLOR PALPATINE FROM THE SEPARATISTS

(*Revenge of the Sith*)

In a last-ditch effort to end the Clone Wars, Count Dooku and General Grievous mount an assault on the Republic's capital planet to kidnap Chancellor Palpatine. Jedi Knights Anakin Skywalker and Obi-Wan Kenobi come to the rescue, once again.

JYN ERSO FROM IMPERIAL PRISON CAMP

(*Rogue One: A Star Wars Story*)

For her many crimes, Jyn Erso wound up in a desolate Imperial prison camp on Wobani. A rebel team including K-2SO break her out in exchange for valuable intelligence.

A

B

CLOUD CITY
(*The Empire Strikes Back*)

Though he was forced to betray them earlier, Lando saves Leia and Chewbacca from the Empire by helping them escape from Cloud City to fight another day.

HAN SOLO FROM JABBA THE HUTT
(*Return of the Jedi*)

Han's luck runs out when he is frozen in carbonite and hung on Jabba's wall as decoration. Leia uses a disguise to stage his rescue. (**Image B**)

POE DAMERON'S FIRST ORDER CAPTURE
(*The Force Awakens*)

Luckily for Poe Dameron, a nearby First Order stormtrooper has a sudden change of heart. That trooper, now known as Finn, breaks the pilot out and the duo make their escape from Kylo Ren's Star Destroyer. (**Image C**)

ROSE TICO'S RESCUE OF FINN
(*The Last Jedi*)

Rose's intervention at the Battle of Crait saves Finn from foolishly sacrificing himself to the First Order.

PRINCESS LEIA ABOARD THE DEATH STAR
(*A New Hope*)

When captured by the Empire and held prisoner on a moon-sized space station, Leia wasn't expecting to be rescued. Fortunately, Luke, Han, and Obi-Wan stumbled upon the Death Star just in time to save her (and the entire galaxy).

C

76

POMP AND CIRCUMSTANCE

THE AWARD CEREMONIES, CORONATIONS, AND DISPLAYS OF MILITARY MIGHT

THE BEST EVENTS IN *STAR WARS* HAVE A SENSE OF EPIC SCALE AND THESE EVENTS ARE NO EXCEPTION. THESE AWARD CEREMONIES AND DISPLAYS OF MILITARY MIGHT REMIND US OF THE HIGH STAKES INVOLVED IN THE STRUGGLE BETWEEN GOOD AND EVIL. THEY ALSO BEGIN TO CONVEY THE MAGNITUDE OF THE CONFLICT WE SEE ON SCREEN.

A

B

C

NABOO PEACE PARADE
(*The Phantom Menace*) **(Image A)**

QUI-GON JINN'S FUNERAL
(*The Phantom Menace*)

GRAND ARMY OF THE REPUBLIC ON DISPLAY
(*Attack of the Clones*)

ANAKIN SKYWALKER AND PADMÉ AMIDALA'S WEDDING
(*Attack of the Clones*)

SUPREME CHANCELLOR PALPATINE DECLARES HIMSELF EMPEROR
(*Revenge of the Sith*)

PADMÉ AMIDALA'S FUNERAL
(*Revenge of the Sith*)

YAVIN MEDAL CEREMONY
(*A New Hope*) **(Image B)**

EMPEROR PALPATINE'S ARRIVAL
(*Return of the Jedi*)

EMPEROR PALPATINE'S FALL
(*Return of the Jedi*)

GENERAL ARMITAGE HUX'S SPEECH
(*The Force Awakens*) **(Image C)**

THE SITH FLEET RISING
(*The Rise of Skywalker*) **(Image D)**

D

77

BOOM!

THE BIGGEST BATTLE EXPLOSIONS

THE MOST SATISFYING CONCLUSION TO ANY EPIC BATTLE IS AN EPIC EXPLOSION! THE DESTRUCTION OF THE DEATH STAR IN *A New Hope* SET THE STANDARD FOR A GREAT DETONATION, AND THEY'VE ONLY GROWN BIGGER AS THE YEARS GO ON.

TRADE FEDERATION CONTROL SHIP
(*The Phantom Menace*)

BATTLE OF CORUSCANT
(*Revenge of the Sith*)

VANDOR
(*Solo: A Star Wars Story*) (**Image A**)

SCARIF SHIELDGATE
(*Rogue One: A Star Wars Story*) (**Image B**)

DEATH STAR EXPLOSION
(*A New Hope*) (**Image C**)

DEATH STAR II EXPLOSION
(*Return of the Jedi*)

ENDOR SHIELD GENERATOR
(*Return of the Jedi*) (**Image D**)

HOSNIAN PRIME
(*The Force Awakens*)

STARKILLER BASE
(*The Force Awakens*)

THE *SUPREMACY*
(*The Last Jedi*) (**Image E**)

THE SITH ETERNAL COMMAND SHIP
(*The Rise of Skywalker*)

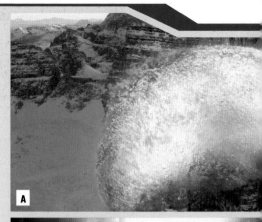

A

B

E

CHAPTER 7:
GALACTIC
MISCELLANY

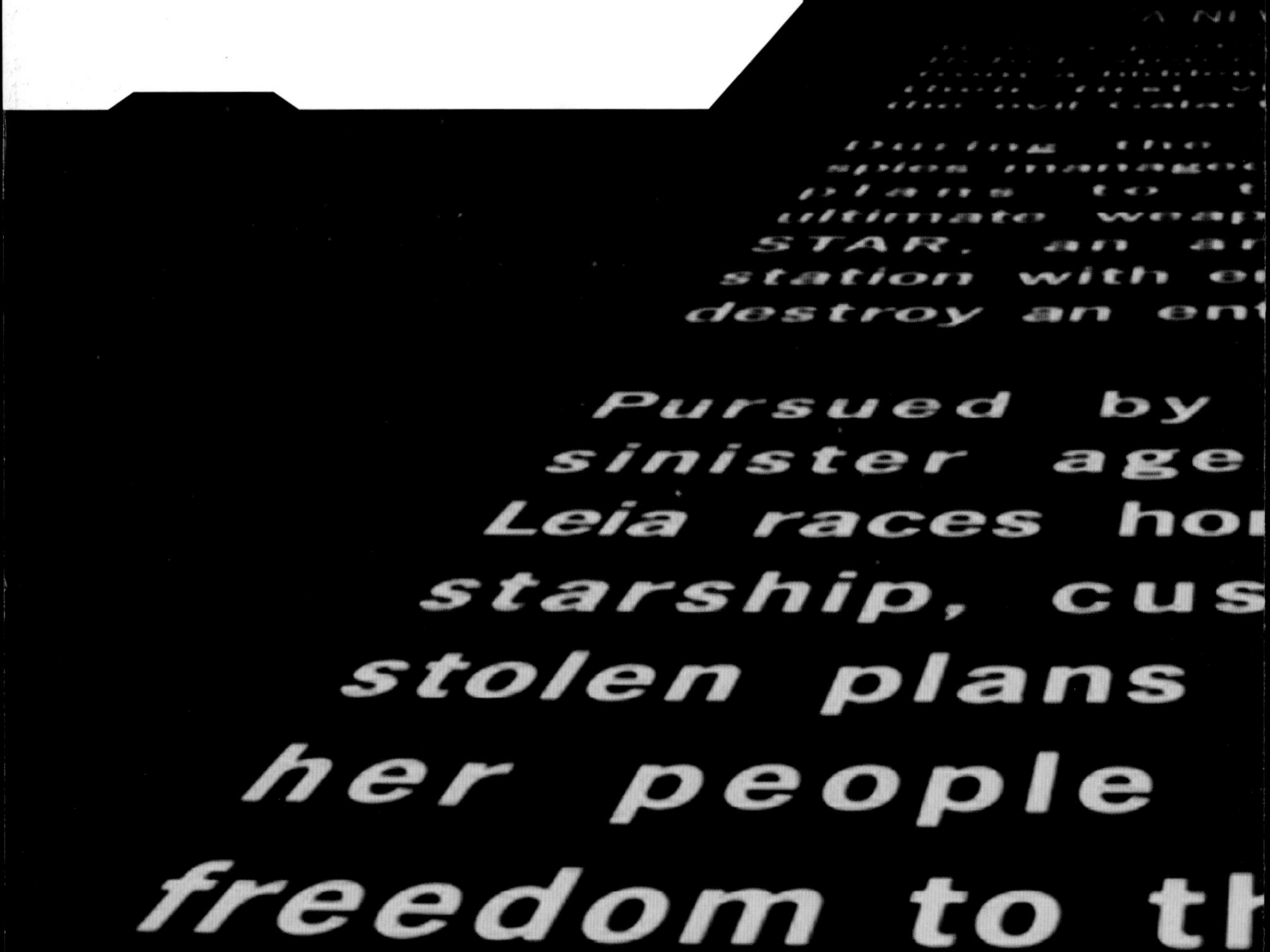

A N[...]

[...]
[...]
[...]

During the
spies managed
plans to [...]
ultimate weap[...]
STAR, an ar[...]
station with e[...]
destroy an en[...]

Pursued by
sinister age[...]
Leia races ho[...]
starship, cus[...]
stolen plans
her people
freedom to t[...]

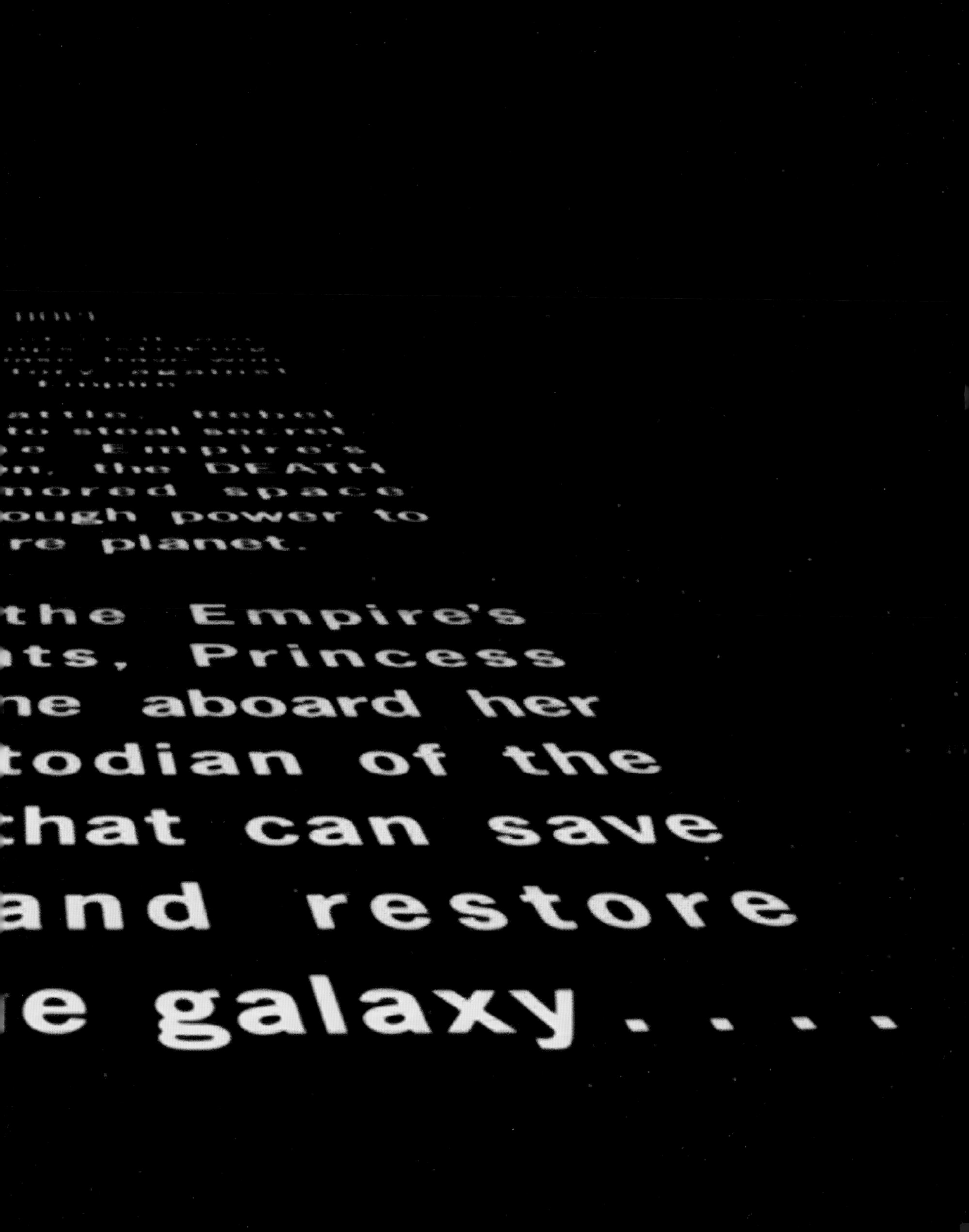

...l...
...in...
...ith
...ry against
...Lnplin

...attle, Rebel
...to steal secret
...e Empire's
...n, the DEATH
...mored space
...ough power to
...re planet.

...the Empire's
...ts, Princess
...he aboard her
...todian of the
...hat can save
...and restore
...e galaxy....

78

TELL ME THE ODDS

THE VARIOUS ODDS THAT C-3PO QUOTES

ONE WAY TO PORTRAY THE DANGER AHEAD IS TO LITERALLY SAY HOW HIGH THE ODDS ARE STACKED AGAINST THE CHARACTERS. DROIDS ARE PARTICULARLY ADEPT AT CALCULATING—AND PROCLAIMING—THE ODDS FACED IN A GIVEN SITUATION, WHETHER IT BE THE WORRISOME C-3PO OR THE MATTER-OF-FACT K-2SO.

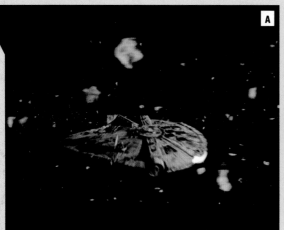

A

B

SUCCESSFULLY NAVIGATING AN ASTEROID FIELD IN THE *MILLENNIUM FALCON*:

approximately 3,720 to 1

(Image A)

SURVIVING OVERNIGHT IN A HOTH SNOWSTORM:

725 to 1

(Image B)

MAKING THE SHOT TO DESTROY THE DEATH STAR:

1,000,000 to 1

(Image C)

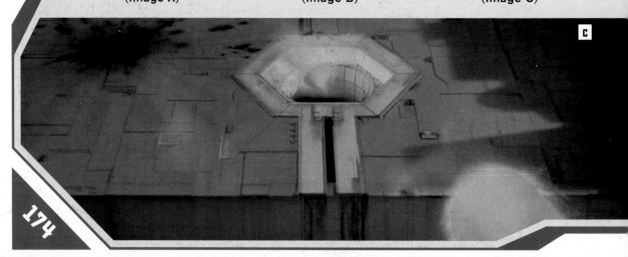

C

K-2SO'S PROJECTED PROBABILITY THAT JYN ERSO WILL USE A BLASTER AGAINST CASSIAN ANDOR:

"It's high. Very high."

(Image D)

CHANCE THAT ROGUE ONE WILL FAIL TO SECURE THE DEATH STAR PLANS ON SCARIF:

97.6%

(Image E)

79

"LIES! DECEPTIONS!"

CHARACTERS AND THEIR BIGGEST LIES

In his later years, Rebel partisan Saw Gerrera is paranoid that everyone will betray him. Given how long this list of lies is, perhaps he was onto something. From scheming Sith to sneaky smugglers, these are the biggest liars and their mistruths.

QUI-GON JINN CHECKING ANAKIN SKYWALKER'S BLOOD

(The Phantom Menace)

Jedi Qui-Gon Jinn suspects that the young slave boy Anakin is strong with the Force, but can't be sure without a blood test. He sneakily takes a sample for analysis, telling him that he's cleaning a scrape.

CHANCELLOR PALPATINE'S LOVE OF DEMOCRACY

(Attack of the Clones)

When handed emergency powers by the Galactic Senate, then-Chancellor Palpatine declares that he "loves democracy" and also loves "the Senate." He eventually destroys both from the inside. **(Image A)**

EMPEROR PALPATINE'S LIE TO VADER

(Revenge of the Sith)

The first sign of a bad boss might be when he tells you that you killed your wife in a fit of rage. It's just one of many manipulative lies Palpatine feeds to Darth Vader during his troubled apprenticeship.

HAN SOLO'S KESSEL RUN IN "LESS THAN 12 PARSECS"

(Solo: A Star Wars Story)

Han Solo's flying through the deadly maelstrom around Kessel is an impressive feat at any speed, but the smuggler can't help but round down when bragging about his record time.

TOBIAS BECKETT'S BETRAYAL

(Solo: A Star Wars Story)

When Han Solo and Qi'ra decide to help Enfys Nest's rebellion by giving them the coaxium owed to Dryden Vos, Beckett betrays them to save his own neck.

HAN SOLO'S "THERMAL DETONATOR"

(Solo: A Star Wars Story)

The scrappy scrumrat Han escapes punishment from his criminal bosses by pretending he's holding a thermal detonator. The ruse doesn't last long, as Lady Proxima quickly recognizes the "detonator" is just a rock. **(Image B)**

A

B

CASSIAN'S MISSION TO KILL GALEN ERSO
(*Rogue One: A Star Wars Story*)

Cassian Andor doesn't mention to Jyn Erso why they are traveling to a secret science facility where Jyn's father is working on the Death Star superlaser. Jyn thinks it's a rescue mission, but Cassian has other orders.

PRINCESS LEIA'S ATTEMPT TO DECEIVE GRAND MOFF TARKIN
(*A New Hope*)

Even with the threat of the destruction of her home world looming, Leia Organa refuses to give up the location of the Rebel Alliance's hidden base on Yavin 4. She instead gives Grand Moff Tarkin and Darth Vader the location of an abandoned base on Dantooine.

UNCLE OWEN MISLEADING LUKE ABOUT OBI-WAN KENOBI'S EXISTENCE
(*A New Hope*)

Perhaps Owen Lars just wants to protect his nephew when he tells Luke that Obi-Wan Kenobi is dead. Though aging and in hiding, Obi-Wan is far from gone.

EMPEROR PALPATINE'S TRAP
(*Return of the Jedi*)

Palpatine thinks he has the Rebel Alliance trapped at the Battle of Endor, having fed the Alliance misinformation about the second Death Star. The Rebels arrive thinking the battle station is not yet operational, a mistake they realize when the station's turbolaser begins firing on their fleet.

DJ'S BETRAYAL
(*The Last Jedi*)

Who would have through that a scoundrel met in a jail cell wouldn't be the most trustworthy partner? Finn and Rose discover that the slicer is willing to sell them to the First Order to save his own life. Afterall, to DJ, it's just business. (**Image C**)

KYLO REN TURNS ON SUPREME LEADER SNOKE
(*The Last Jedi*)

The dark side of the Force gives Supreme Leader Snoke heightened senses, but he misjudges his apprentice's loyalty. Ren pretends to be a loyal apprentice, kills Snoke, and takes the title of Supreme Leader for himself.

SNEAKY DISGUISES

HEROES WHO HAVE DRESSED AS IMPERIALS, BOUNTY HUNTERS, OR OTHERS TO EVADE SOMEONE

Though some prefer a straight blaster fight to sneaking around, there's no arguing that a good disguise goes a long way during a dangerous infiltration mission. These are the heroes who hide in plain sight.

A

PADMÉ AMIDALA AS A HANDMAIDEN
(*The Phantom Menace*)
Padmé's disguise as a handmaiden to the queen is so convincing that even Jedi Qui-Gon Jinn and Obi-Wan Kenobi fall for the trick. Little do they realize that she *is* the queen.

TOBIAS BECKETT'S CREW AS IMPERIALS
(*Solo: One A Star Wars Story*)
Needing to steal an Imperial lifter for the upcoming train heist, Beckett and his crew take Imperial soldier uniforms on Mimban. They casually scout for their target while hiding in plain sight.

TOBIAS BECKETT AS A GUARD
(*Solo: A Star Wars Story*)
Beckett accompanies Qi'ra masquerading as a security guard to gain access to the Kessel mine control room in their ruse to steal coaxium hyperfuel.

JYN ERSO AND CASSIAN ANDOR AS IMPERIALS
(*Rogue One: A Star Wars Story*)
Jyn and Cassian pull a similar stunt to Luke and Han when they ambush the Imperials who come to inspect their ship. Taking their uniforms, Jyn and Cassian can walk right into one of the most secure Imperial installations. K-2SO, being a former Imperial droid, needs no disguise to blend in with the crowd.

80

LUKE SKYWALKER AND HAN SOLO AS STORMTROOPERS
(*A New Hope*)

Luke and Han lure two unsuspecting stormtroopers aboard the *Millennium Falcon* to steal their helmeted armor. Even though the outfit is a little ill-fitting for the height-challenged Luke, the armor is a passable enough disguise to allow them to make their way through the Death Star corridors.

PRINCESS LEIA AS BOUSHH
(*Return of the Jedi*)

How do you infiltrate a crime lord's castle outfitted with a giant gate, brutish guards, and packed with bounty hunters? Sneak in disguised as a bounty hunter yourself. With the suit's built in voice changer, Leia gets in without a fight. (**Image A**)

LANDO CALRISSIAN AS A GUARD
(*Return of the Jedi*)

Lando prepares for Han Solo's rescue by posing as a guard. He uses a disguise that spent years stashed away aboard the *Millennium Falcon*. It's the same armor Beckett used years before on Kessel. (**Image B**)

FINN AND ROSE TICO AS FIRST ORDER OFFICERS
(*The Last Jedi*)

Using Finn's knowledge of the ship, the heroic

C

duo sneaks onboard Snoke's flagship to hack the ship's hyperspace tracker with the help of the slicer, DJ.

BB-8 AS A TRASHCAN
(*The Last Jedi*)

BB-8 accompanies Finn and Rose on their mission to infiltrate Snoke's flagship. While the humans wear First Order uniforms, BB-8 settles for an upside-down trash can to make him look like a droid. To really sell the disguise, BB-8 even does his best impression of mouse droid beeps. (**Image C**)

LANDO CALRISSIAN AS THE HERMIT
(*The Rise of Skywalker*)

In the decades after the fall of the Empire, personal tragedy leads Lando Calrissian take up a hermit's life on Pasaana. Disguised in a Taloraan Wind Raider's helmet, he dares not reveal his identity to the locals for fear that old enemies might find him. (**Image D**)

B

81

FROM WICKET TO WEAZEL

WARWICK DAVIS AND HIS CHARACTERS WHO START WITH A "W"

ACTOR WARWICK DAVIS BEGAN HIS ACTING CAREER IN 1983'S *RETURN OF THE JEDI*, PORTRAYING THE EWOK WICKET. SINCE THEN, IT HAS BECOME A TRADITION FOR DAVIS TO PORTRAY OTHER CHARACTERS IN *STAR WARS* FILMS, ALL WITH NAMES THAT BEGIN WITH "W." THE TRADITION EXTENDS FURTHER THAN *STAR WARS* TOO, AS DAVIS PORTRAYED THE TITULAR CHARACTER IN THE 1988 LUCASFILM FEATURE, *WILLOW*. FROM EWOKS TO SCOUNDRELS TO DROIDS, THESE ARE SOME OF THE MANY CHARACTERS PLAYED BY WARWICK DAVIS.

WEAZEL
(*The Phantom Menace, Solo: A Star Wars Story*)

WALD
(*The Phantom Menace*)

WEAZEL
(*Solo: A Star Wars Story*)

W1-EG5
(*Solo: A Star Wars Story*)

WG-22
(*Solo: A Star Wars Story*)

WAZELLMAN
(*Solo: A Star Wars Story*)

WG-22
(*Solo: A Star Wars Story*)

WICKET
(*Return of the Jedi*)

WOLLIVAN
(*The Force Awakens*)

82

LOST LIMBS
CHRONICLE OF SEVERED BODY PARTS

IT'S SAID THAT LIGHTSABERS ARE ELEGANT WEAPONS FROM A MORE CIVILIZED AGE. YET FOR ALL THEIR ELEGANCE, IT SEEMS THAT OFTEN WHEN SOMEONE BRANDISHES A LIGHTSABER, SOMEONE ELSE LOSES A LIMB. HANDS, ARMS, LEGS, AND HEADS: NO EXTREMITY IS SAFE—ESPECIALLY IF YOU'RE A SKYWALKER!

DARTH MAUL'S LOWER HALF
(*The Phantom Menace*)

Darth Maul prepares his whole life to fight the Jedi, but he isn't prepared for a scrappy young Obi-Wan Kenobi. During their duel on Naboo, Kenobi catches Maul off guard and slices him in half. Maul looks stunned as his lower half tumbles down the abyss right behind his upper half. (**Image A**)

ZAM WESELL'S RIGHT ARM
(*Attack of the Clones*)

Shape-shifting bounty hunter Zam Wesell loses her right arm when she tries to sneak up on Obi-Wan Kenobi in a crowded Coruscant nightclub. It's not the first—or the last—time that Obi-Wan will sever a limb with his lightsaber.

ANAKIN SKYWALKER'S RIGHT FOREARM
(*Attack of the Clones*)

In a vicious and frenzied lightsaber duel with Count Dooku in a Geonosis hanger, Anakin's impetuousness and desire for revenge leads him to over-estimate his abilities. He pays for this by having his right forearm lopped off by the Sith Lord. (**Image B**)

COUNT DOOKU'S HANDS AND HEAD
(*Revenge of the Sith*)

The final film in the prequel trilogy has the distinction of holding the highest lost-limb count in any *Star Wars* film to date. In the film's epic opening battle over Coruscant, Count Dooku gets a taste of his own medicine as Anakin Skywalker severs both of Dooku's hands before finally decapitating him at the urging of Chancellor Palpatine. (**Image C**)

MACE WINDU'S RIGHT ARM
(*Revenge of the Sith*)

The Jedi Master is caught by surprise when Anakin Skywalker slices through his right arm, giving Palpatine the opening he needs to blast Windu out of a window with powerful Force lightning. (**Image D**)

ANAKIN SKYWALKER'S LEFT ARM AND BOTH LEGS
(*Revenge of the Sith*)

Having already lost his right forearm in a duel with Count Dooku, Skywalker loses his remaining limbs in his fateful fight against his former master, Obi-Wan Kenobi. Hideously scarred and broken from the experience, he lives out the rest of his life encased in armor as Darth Vader, equipped with various mechanical limbs and an assortment of life support systems. (**Image E**)

PYKE SYNDICATE GUARD'S ARMS
(*Solo: A Star Wars Story*)

During their heist on Kessel, Han Solo learns first hand that Chewbacca can pull someone's arms clean off when he's upset.

PONDA BABA'S RIGHT ARM
(*A New Hope*)

Alongside his business partner Dr. Evazan, Ponda Baba is an ill-tempered alien always looking for a fight. But when he takes offense to Luke Skywalker in a Mos Eisley Cantina, this confrontational criminal walks out of the bar with one less arm than he came in with thanks to some deft lightsaber work from Obi-Wan Kenobi. (**Image F**)

LUKE SKYWALKER'S RIGHT HAND
(*The Empire Strikes Back*)

When Luke Skywalker confronts Darth Vader on Bespin's Cloud City, the former farm boy soon realizes he is extremely outmatched. Not wanting to kill Luke, Vader instead disarms the young Jedi by severing his hand, lightsaber and all. To add insult to injury, Luke then learns the shocking truth that Vader is actually his dad! Like father, like son, lost limbs now run in the Skywalker family. (**Image G**)

DARTH VADER'S MECHANICAL RIGHT HAND
(*Return of the Jedi*)

During their rematch on the second Death Star during the Battle of Endor, Luke returns the favor and severs his father's mechanical right hand in anger. Realizing he is in danger of following in Vader's footsteps, Luke tosses his lightsaber aside and refuses to fight. (*Image H*)

83

"I HAVE A BAD FEELING ABOUT THIS"

ALL THE TIMES CHARACTERS HAVE UTTERED THIS LINE

IT HAS BECOME TRADITION IN *STAR WARS* FILMS FOR A CHARACTER TO SAY "I HAVE A BAD FEELING ABOUT THIS," AS THE HEROES HEAD INTO A DANGEROUS SITUATION. THE MOST NOTABLE EXCEPTION IS HAN'S STATEMENT IN *SOLO: A STAR WARS STORY*, WHERE THE YOUNG SCOUNDREL NAIVELY PROCLAIMS HE HAS "A GOOD FEELING ABOUT THIS" BEFORE MAKING THE LIFE-THREATENING KESSEL RUN. THAT POSITIVE OUTLOOK MELTS AWAY BY THE TIME WE SEE THE CHARACTER IN *A NEW HOPE*. IN THE END, HE MUTTERS THE FAMOUS LINE MORE THAN ANYONE ELSE.

OBI-WAN KENOBI
(*The Phantom Menace*)
Upon arriving for negotiations with the Trade Federation.

ANAKIN SKYWALKER
(*Attack of the Clones*)
As he faces execution in the Geonosis arena. (**Image A**)

OBI-WAN KENOBI
(*Revenge of the Sith*)
When attempting to crash land on a Separatist capital ship.

HAN SOLO
(*Solo: A Star Wars Story*)

K-2SO
(*Rogue One: A Star Wars Story*)
As he infiltrates an Imperial stronghold. (**Image B**)

LUKE SKYWALKER
(*A New Hope*)
On approach to the Death Star.

HAN SOLO
(*A New Hope*)
When stuck in the Death Star trash compactor.

LEIA ORGANA
(*The Empire Strikes Back*)
Suspicious as the *Millennium Falcon* seemingly lands in an asteroid field. (**Image C**)

C-3PO
(*Return of the Jedi*)
Entering Jabba the Hutt's Palace.

HAN SOLO
(*Return of the Jedi*)
Captured by Ewoks on Endor.
(**Image D**)

HAN SOLO
(*The Force Awakens*)
Realizing that rathtars are on the loose.

BB-8
(*The Last Jedi*)
Facing the First Order fleet in a lone X-wing with Poe.

LANDO CALRISSIAN
(*The Rise of Skywalker*)

A

B

C

D

84

WHO SAID THAT?

MATCH THE FAMOUS DIALOGUE TO ITS SPEAKER

Can you match these nine famous quotes to their speaker? Test your knowledge with this list of must-know lines from the films.

1
"NO, I AM YOUR FATHER."

2
"IT'S A TRAP!"

3
"DO OR DO NOT, THERE IS NO TRY."

4
"HELP ME OBI-WAN KENOBI, YOU'RE MY ONLY HOPE."

5
"NOW THIS IS PODRACING"

6
"SO THIS IS HOW LIBERTY DIES. WITH THUNDEROUS APPLAUSE."

7
"CHEWIE, WE'RE HOME."

8
"I'M ONE WITH THE FORCE. THE FORCE IS WITH ME."

9
"I AM A JEDI, LIKE MY FATHER BEFORE ME."

1F, 2E, 3H, 4C, 5G, 6I, 7D, 8B, 9A

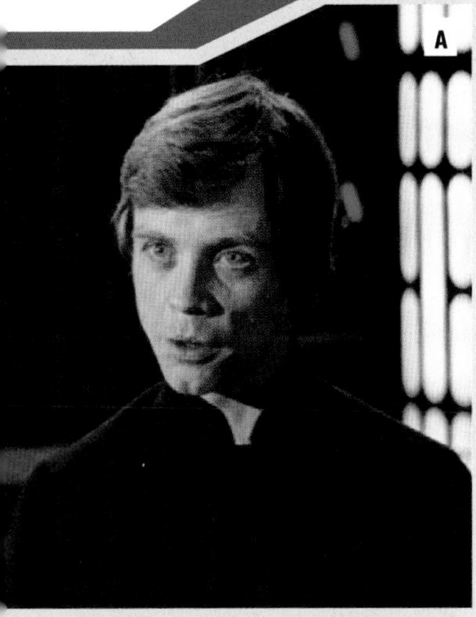
A

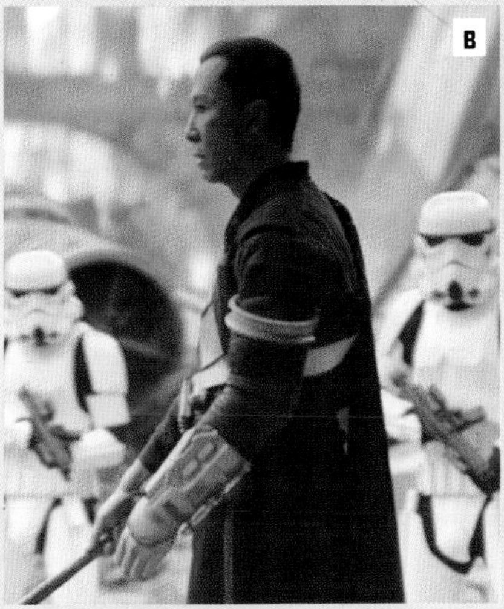
B

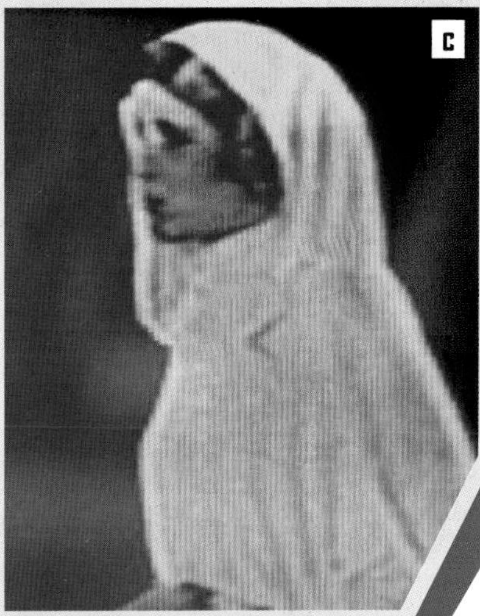
C

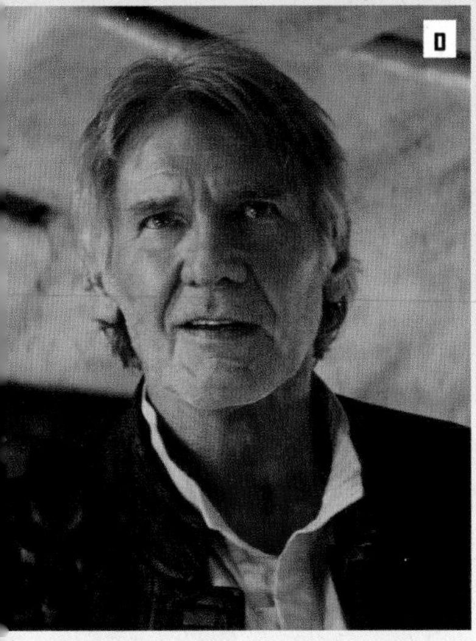
D

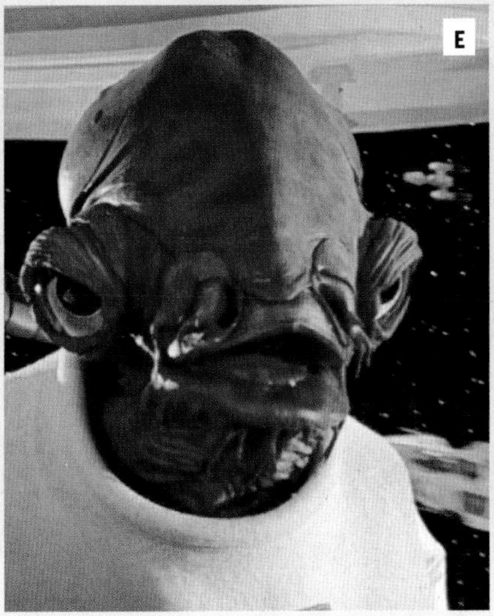
E

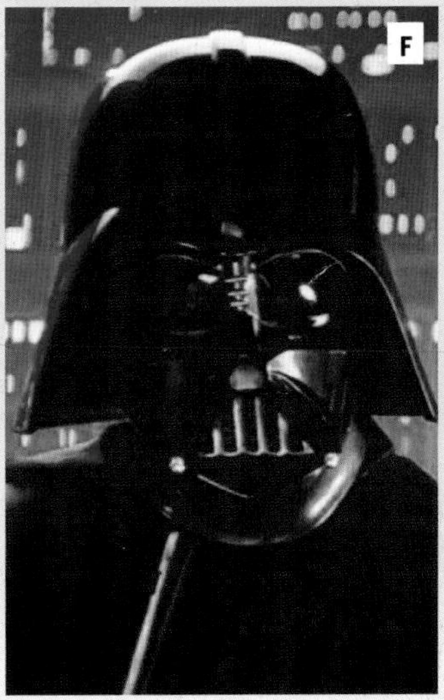
F

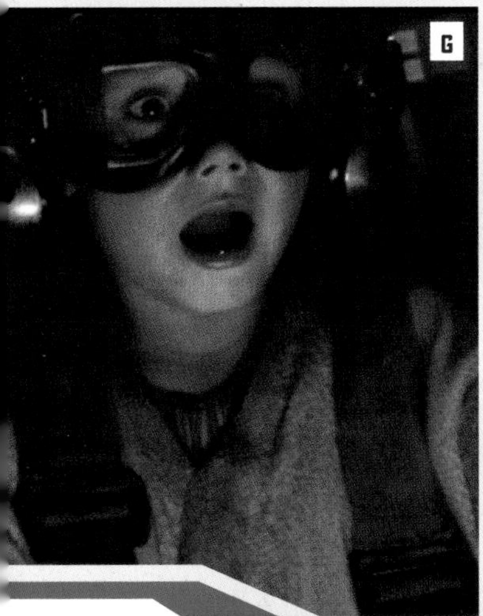
G

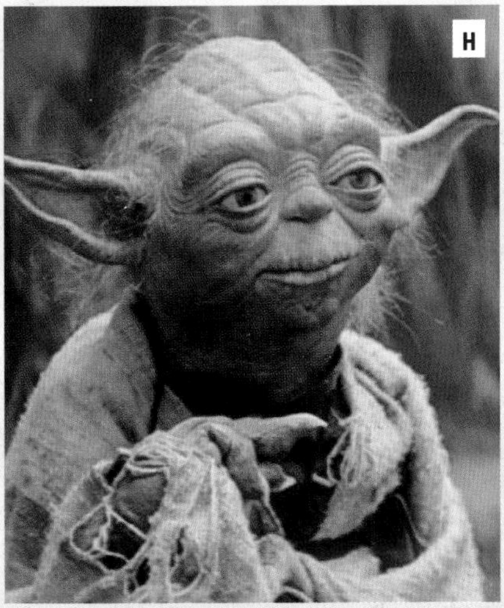
H

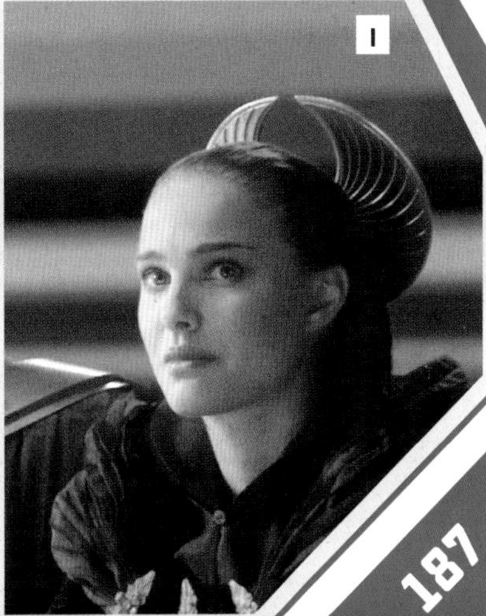
I

85

ROLL IT
OPENING SCROLLS OF THE SAGA

Styled after the classic film serials of the 1930s and 1940s, the opening crawl of the saga films sets the stage for the film, quickly explaining the situation before throwing audiences into the action.

EPISODE I
THE PHANTOM MENACE

Turmoil has engulfed the Galactic Republic. The taxation of trade routes to outlying star systems is in dispute.
Hoping to resolve the matter with a blockade of deadly battleships, the greedy Trade Federation has stopped all shipping to the small planet of Naboo.

While the Congress of the Republic endlessly debates this alarming chain of events, the Supreme Chancellor has secretly dispatched two Jedi Knights, the guardians of peace and justice in the galaxy, to settle the conflict . . . .

EPISODE II
ATTACK OF THE CLONES

There is unrest in the Galactic Senate. Several thousand solar systems have declared their intentions to leave the Republic.

This separatist movement, under the leadership of the mysterious Count Dooku, has made it difficult for the limited number of Jedi Knights to maintain peace and order in the galaxy.
Senator Amidala, the former Queen of Naboo, is returning to the Galactic Senate to vote on the critical issue of creating an ARMY OF THE REPUBLIC to assist the overwhelmed Jedi . . . .

EPISODE III
REVENGE OF THE SITH

War! The Republic is crumbling under attacks by the ruthless Sith Lord, Count Dooku. There are heroes on both sides. Evil is everywhere.

In a stunning move, the fiendish droid leader, General Grievous, has swept into the Republic capital and kidnapped Chancellor Palpatine, leader of the Galactic Senate.

As the Separatist Droid Army attempts to flee the besieged capital with their valuable hostage, two Jedi Knights lead a desperate mission to rescue the captive Chancellor . . . .

EPISODE IV
A NEW HOPE

It is a period of civil war. Rebel spaceships, striking from a hidden base, have won their first victory against the evil Galactic Empire.

During the battle, Rebel spies managed to steal secret plans to the Empire's ultimate weapon, the DEATH STAR, an armored space station with enough power to destroy an entire planet.

Pursued by the Empire's sinister agents, Princess Leia races home aboard her starship, custodian of the stolen plans that can save her people and restore freedom to the galaxy . . . .

EPISODE V
THE EMPIRE STRIKES BACK

It is a dark time for the Rebellion. Although the Death Star has been destroyed, Imperial troops have driven the Rebel forces from their hidden base and pursued them across the galaxy.

Evading the dreaded Imperial Starfleet, a group of freedom fighters led by Luke Skywalker has established a new secret base on the remote ice world of Hoth.

It is a period of civil war.
Rebel spaceships, striking
from a hidden base, have won
their first victory against
the evil Galactic Empire.

During the battle, Rebel
spies managed to steal secret
plans to the Empire's
ultimate weapon, the DEATH
STAR, an armored space
station with enough power to
destroy an entire planet.

Pursued by the Empire's
sinister agents, Princess
Leia races home aboard her
starship, custodian of the
stolen plans that can save
her people and restore
freedom to the galaxy . . . .

The evil lord Darth Vader, obsessed with finding young Skywalker, has dispatched thousands of remote probes into the far reaches of space . . . .

EPISODE VI
RETURN OF THE JEDI

Luke Skywalker has returned to his home planet of Tatooine in an attempt to rescue his friend Han Solo from the clutches of the vile gangster Jabba the Hutt.

Little does Luke know that the GALACTIC EMPIRE has secretly begun construction on a new armored space station even more powerful than the first dreaded Death Star.

When completed, this ultimate weapon will spell certain doom for the small band of rebels struggling to restore freedom to the galaxy . . . .

EPISODE VII
THE FORCE AWAKENS

Luke Skywalker has vanished. In his absence, the sinister FIRST ORDER has risen from the ashes of the Empire and will not rest until Skywalker, the last Jedi, has been destroyed.

With the support of the REPUBLIC, General Leia Organa leads a brave RESISTANCE. She is desperate to find her brother Luke and gain his help in restoring peace and justice to the galaxy.

Leia has sent her most daring pilot on a secret mission to Jakku, where an old ally has discovered a clue to Luke's whereabouts . . . .

EPISODE VIII
THE LAST JEDI

The FIRST ORDER reigns. Having decimated the peaceful Republic, Supreme Leader Snoke now deploys the merciless legions to seize military control of the galaxy.

Only General Leia Organa's band of RESISTANCE fighters stand against the rising tyranny, certain that Jedi Master Luke Skywalker will return and restore a spark of hope to the fight.

But the Resistance has been exposed. As the First Order speeds toward the rebel base, the brave heroes mount a desperate escape . . . .

EPISODE IX
THE RISE OF SKYWALKER

The dead speak! The galaxy has heard a mysterious broadcast, a threat of REVENGE in the sinister voice of the late EMPEROR PALPATINE.

GENERAL LEIA ORGANA dispatches secret agents to gather intelligence, while REY, the last hope of the Jedi, trains for battle against the diabolical FIRST ORDER.

Meanwhile, Supreme Leader KYLO REN rages in search of the phantom Emperor, determined to destroy any threat to his power . . . .

86

K-I-S-S

ALL THE ROMANTIC, FRIENDLY, AND AWKWARD KISSES

SOME ARE ROMANTIC, SOME ARE FRIENDLY, AND IN THE CASE OF LUKE AND LEIA, SOME ARE DOWNRIGHT AWKWARD. THESE ARE THE TIMES WHERE CHARACTERS LOCK LIPS.

ANAKIN SKYWALKER AND PADMÉ AMIDALA
(Attack of the Clones)

PADMÉ AMIDALA AND ANAKIN SKYWALKER
(Attack of the Clones)

ANAKIN SKYWALKER AND PADMÉ AMIDALA
(Revenge of the Sith)

PADMÉ AMIDALA AND ANAKIN SKYWALKER
(Revenge of the Sith)

HAN SOLO AND QI'RA
(Solo: A Star Wars Story)

PRINCESS LEIA AND LUKE SKYWALKER
(A New Hope)

PRINCESS LEIA AND LUKE SKYWALKER
(*The Empire Strikes Back*)

HAN SOLO AND PRINCESS LEIA
(*The Empire Strikes Back*)

HAN SOLO AND PRINCESS LEIA
(*The Empire Strikes Back*)

PRINCESS LEIA AND HAN SOLO
(*Return of the Jedi*)

PRINCESS LEIA AND HAN SOLO
(*Return of the Jedi*)

FINN AND ROSE TICO
(*The Last Jedi*)

87

HIDE AND SEEK

CLEVER PLACES WHERE OUR HEROES HAVE HIDDEN FROM THE ENEMY

WITH A VILLAIN NOT FAR BEHIND, A CLEVER HIDING SPOT IS OFTEN THE DIFFERENCE BETWEEN LIFE AND DEATH. THE SAGA FEATURES MANY OF THESE HIGH-STAKES GAMES OF HIDE AND SEEK, SHOWCASING OUR HEROES' INGENUITY AND QUICK THINKING IN STRESSFUL SITUATIONS.

R2-D2'S DESERT ESCAPE
(*A New Hope*)

R2-D2 evades marauding Tusken Raiders in a rocky overhang when they attack Luke and C-3PO. His hiding ensures he is the only one to come away from the encounter unscathed.

MOS EISLEY'S DISAPPEARING DROIDS
(*A New Hope*)

As Imperial troopers patrol the streets of Mos Eisley in search of R2-D2 and C-3PO, the pair act quickly to hide inside a nearby building. Though C-3PO isn't normally one for breaking the rules, his programming for self-preservation kicks in just in time. (**Image A**)

DEATH STAR DROIDS
(*A New Hope*)

While the other heroes venture out into the Death Star on their mission to find Princess Leia, R2-D2 and C-3PO stay behind to hide in a control room closet. When discovered, C-3PO yet again displays a penchant for telling lies when his own wellbeing is on the line. He makes up quite a convincing story to get past the guards.

CONVENIENT COMPARTMENTS
(*A New Hope*)

Han Solo maintains a set of secret compartments in the floor of the *Millennium Falcon* for smuggling illicit goods. He never expects he will someday hide inside them, but that's just what happens when the ship is captured by the Death Star. The Imperial soldiers are fooled by a seemingly empty ship, not knowing that the fugitives sit just below their feet.

MILLENNIUM FALCON DISAPPEARING ACT
(*The Empire Strikes Back*)

With his hyperdrive acting up, Han evades an Imperial fleet by attaching his ship to the bridge of a Star Destroyer and powering down. They have no idea that a ship full of Rebels is hiding right behind their backs. (**Image B**)

B

FINN AND REY IN HIDING
(*The Force Awakens*)

On the run and in over their heads, Rey and Finn spend much of their time after leaving Jakku trying to avoid more trouble. First when their stolen freighter (the *Millennium Falcon*) is captured and shortly thereafter when discovered by Kanjiklub and the Guavian Death Gang, they find a place to hide in the passageways underneath freighter floors.

AHCH-TO
(*The Force Awakens*, *The Last Jedi*)

Luke himself calls the planet Ahch-To "the most unfindable place in the galaxy." Luke hides so well on this little-known planet that even his family doesn't know his location. The same goes for the First Order, who are hunting the Jedi Master in hopes of eliminating the last of the Jedi Order. (**Image C**)

C

SWITCHING SIDES
DEFECTORS AND TRAITORS

WHETHER THEY HAVE A CHANGE OF HEART OR ARE LURED TO THE DARK SIDE, THE CHOICES THESE DEFECTORS AND TRAITORS MAKE HAS A PROFOUND IMPACT ON GALACTIC HISTORY. A LITTLE DISLOYALTY GOES A LONG WAY TO UPSETTING THE BALANCE BETWEEN GOOD AND EVIL.

A

COUNT DOOKU
(*Attack of the Clones*)
Abandons the Jedi Order and becomes a Sith.

ANAKIN SKYWALKER
(*Revenge of the Sith*)
Betrays the Jedi Order to join the Sith. (**Image A**)

EMPEROR PALPATINE
(*Revenge of the Sith*)
Betrays the Galactic Republic to announce his Galactic Empire. (**Image B**)

HAN SOLO
(*Solo: A Star Wars Story*)
Deserts the Imperial infantry to become a smuggler.

GALEN ERSO
(*Rogue One: A Star Wars Story*)
Undermines the Empire to reveal a flaw in the Death Star.

FINN
(*The Force Awakens*)
Betrays the First Order to join the Resistance. (**Image C**)

DJ
(*The Last Jedi*)
Betrays Finn and Rose Tico to the First Order. (*Image D*)

BEN SOLO
(*The Last Jedi*)
Abandons the Jedi Order for the dark side.

ALL IN THE FAMILY
PARENTS AND THEIR NOTABLE OFFSPRING

SURE, WE ALL KNOW WHO LUKE'S FATHER IS, BUT WHAT ABOUT ALL OF THE OTHER FAMOUS FAMILIES IN THE GALAXY? FAMILY CONNECTIONS WERE PARTICULARLY EXPLORED IN *ATTACK OF THE CLONES*, AS PADMÉ AMIDALA RETURNS HOME TO HER PARENTS, ANAKIN SKYWALKER FOLLOWS THE FORCE IN SEARCH OF HIS MOTHER, AND ANAKIN LEARNS THAT HE HAS EXTENDED FAMILY BACK ON TATOOINE.

A

SHMI SKYWALKER AND SON, ANAKIN
(*The Phantom Menace*) **(Image A)**

JANGO FETT AND CLONED SON, BOBA
(*Attack of the Clones*) **(Image B)**

CLIEGG LARS AND SON, OWEN
(*Attack of the Clones*)

RUWEE AND JOBAL NABERRIE AND DAUGHTER, PADMÉ
(*Attack of the Clones, Revenge of the Sith*)

C

PADMÉ AMIDALA AND ANAKIN SKYWALKER AND TWIN CHILDREN, LUKE AND LEIA
(*Revenge of the Sith*)

GALEN ERSO AND DAUGHTER, JYN
(*Rogue One: A Star Wars Story*)
(Image C)

LEIA ORGANA AND HAN SOLO'S SON, BEN SOLO
(*The Force Awakens*)

EMPEROR PALPATINE AND GRANDDAUGHTER REY
(*The Rise of Skywalker*)

B

WHAT'S IN A NAME

THE MOST UNIQUE *STAR WARS* CHARACTER AND CREATURE NAMES

While most names in *Star Wars* are unique, some names are particularly noteworthy. Whether they are simply creative or have a unique story behind their inception, these are the most distinctive character names the galaxy has to offer.

A

B

C

BEN QUADINAROS
(*The Phantom Menace*)

Quadinaros is a fitting name for an alien who races a pod with four (quad) engines.

YARAEL POOF
(*The Phantom Menace*)

Poof is a fitting name for a character whose head is shaped like a cotton swab. (**Image A**)

OAKIE DOKES
(*Attack of the Clones*)

This member of the Swokes Swokes species is named after *The Phantom Menace's* Live Action Creature Effects Supervisor Nick Dudman's wife, Sue Oakes.

SHU MAI
(*Attack of the Clones*, *Revenge of the Sith*)

This Separatist leader shares a name with a Chinese dumpling.

THERM SCISSORPUNCH
(*Solo: One A Star Wars Story*)

This crustacean-like alien's claws are like scissors, what more is there to say? (**Image B**)

PAODOK'DRABA'TAKAT SAP'DE'REKTI NIK'LINKE'TI' KI'VEF'NIK'NESEVEF'LI'KEK

(*Rogue One: A Star Wars Story*)

Thankfully, this rebel soldier goes by the nickname, Pao. (**Image C**)

CONAN ANTONIO MOTTI

(*A New Hope*)

Motti's first name was given when George Lucas appeared on a 2007 episode of *Late Night with Conan O'Brien*.

JEK PORKINS

(*A New Hope*)

This Rebel pilot, callsign Red Six, happens to be the most corpulent pilot in the squadron.

NIEN NUNB

(*Return of the Jedi, The Force Awakens, The Last Jedi, The Rise of Skywalker*)

First seen in *Return of the Jedi*, this Rebel alien was number nine on a list of behind the scenes production documents. "Number nine" evolved to his official name, Nien Nunb. (**Image D**)

DROOPY MCCOOL

(*Return of the Jedi*)

This is just the stage name for this musician who plays in Jabba's palace.

SALACIOUS B. CRUMB

(*Return of the Jedi*)

Salacious is this monkey-lizard's first name and an accurate description of his personality.

ELLO ASTY

(*The Force Awakens*)

This pilot's name is a reference to the Beastie Boys album, *Hello Nasty*. (**Image E**)

SLOWEN LO

(*The Last Jedi*)

Yet another Beastie Boys reference, this time to their song, "Slow and Low."

DJ

(*The Last Jedi*)

DJ's initials represent his personal mantra: Don't Join.

91

THE GALAXY EXPANDS

MUST-KNOW CHARACTERS FROM LIVE-ACTION, ANIMATION, PARKS, AND PUBLISHING

STAR WARS IS MORE THAN JUST A MOVIE FRANCHISE. NOVELS, COMICS, GAMES, LIVE ACTION SERIES, ANIMATED SERIES, THEME PARKS, AND MORE TELL EXCITING STORIES SET IN A GALAXY FAR, FAR AWAY. THESE STORIES GIVE US A WIDE ARRAY OF NEW CHARACTERS, MANY WHO APPEAR ACROSS MEDIUMS. WHILE IT WOULD BE IMPOSSIBLE TO FIT THEM ALL IN JUST ONE LIST, THESE ARE THE MUST-KNOW CHARACTERS YOU MIGHT HAVE MISSED IF YOU ONLY WATCH THE FILMS.

A

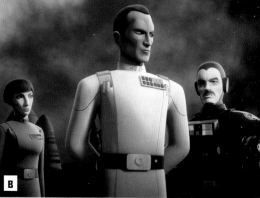

B

C

AHSOKA TANO
(*Star Wars: The Clone Wars* and *Star Wars Rebels*) **(Image A)**

GRAND ADMIRAL THRAWN
(Novels, comics, *Star Wars Rebels*) **(Image B)**

EZRA BRIDGER
(*Star Wars Rebels*) **(Image C)**

KAZ XIONO
(*Star Wars Resistance*)

TAM RYVORA
(*Star Wars Resistance*)

IDEN VERSIO
(*Star Wars:* Battlefront II)

CAL KESTIS
(*Star Wars* Jedi: Fallen Order)

RAE SLOANE
(Novels)

THE GRAND INQUISITOR
(*Star Wars Rebels*, comics, and *Star Wars* Jedi: Fallen Order) **(Image D)**

THE MANDALORIAN
(*Star Wars: The Mandalorian*)

CARA DUNE
(*Star Wars: The Mandalorian*)

GREEF KARGA
(*Star Wars: The Mandalorian*)

DR. APHRA
(Comics)

OGA GARRA
(*Star Wars:* Galaxy's Edge)

DOK-ONDAR
(*Star Wars:* Galaxy's Edge)

VI MORADI
(Novels, *Star Wars:* Galaxy's Edge)

HONDO OHNAKA
(*Star Wars: The Clone Wars*, *Star Wars Rebels*, and *Star Wars:* Galaxy's Edge)
(Image E)

CAPTAIN REX
(*Star Wars: The Clone Wars* and *Star Wars Rebels*)
(Image F)

TRIPLE-ZERO
(Comics)

BEETEE-ONE
(Comics)

THE CHILD
(*Star Wars: The Mandalorian*)

E

F

CHAPTER 8:
BEHIND THE SCENES

92

I KNOW THAT SCREAM

THE FAMOUS WILHELM SCREAM AND WHERE IT'S USED IN EACH *STAR WARS* FILM

ANOTHER RECURRING ELEMENT IN *STAR WARS* IS THE USE A SPECIFIC SOUND EFFECT, KNOWN NOW AS THE WILHELM SCREAM. ITS USE BEGINS WITH SOUND DESIGNER BEN BURTT WHO TOOK NOTE OF DISTINCTIVE SCREAM IN *THE CHARGE AT FEATHER RIVER*, A 1953 WESTERN MOVIE IN WHICH THE CHARACTER PVT. WILHELM MAKES THIS SPECIFIC YELL WHEN INJURED IN BATTLE. BURTT AND OTHER SOUND DESIGNERS MADE IT A POINT TO INCLUDE THE SCREAM IN FILMS THROUGH THE YEARS, THOUGH IT HAS NOW BEEN RETIRED IN FAVOR OF ANOTHER SCREAM IN RECENT INSTALLMENTS.

A

SOLDIERS IN THE THEED HANGAR ON NABOO
(*The Phantom Menace*)

NABOO GUARD CAUGHT BY THE QUEEN'S STARSHIP EXPLOSION
(*Attack of the Clones*) **(Image A)**

CLONE TROOPER DURING THE SPACE BATTLE ABOVE CORUSCANT
(*Revenge of the Sith*)

STORMTROOPERS ON THE DEATH STAR
(*A New Hope*) **(Image B)**

REBEL SOLDIER HIT BY A TURRET EXPLOSION ON HOTH
(*The Empire Strikes Back*)

STORMTROOPER THROWN BY CHEWBACCA IN THE CARBON-FREEZING CHAMBER
(*The Empire Strikes Back*)

SKIFF GUARDS FALLING INTO THE SARLACC PIT
(*Return of the Jedi*)

IMPERIAL OFFICER KNOCKED OVER A RAILING IN THE ENDOR BUNKER
(*Return of the Jedi*) **(Image C)**

FIRST ORDER STORMTROOPER CAUGHT BY AN EXPLOSION ON THE STAR DESTROYER
(*The Force Awakens*)

C

93

WHERE HAVE I SEEN THAT FACE BEFORE?

FAMOUS AND FAMILIAR FACES (AND VOICES)

WHILE THE *STAR WARS* FILMS MADE SOME ACTORS INTO HOUSEHOLD NAMES, SOME ALREADY ESTABLISHED TALENTS HAVE TAKEN ROLES IN THE MOVIES IN A GALAXY FAR, FAR AWAY. WHETHER IT BE RECURRING ROLES OR JUST A CAMEO, THESE ARE SOME OF THE FAMOUS AND FAMILIAR FACES (AND VOICES) FEATURED IN *STAR WARS* FILMS THROUGH THE YEARS.

GREG PROOPS AS THE VOICE OF FODE

(*The Phantom Menace*)

The American actor and comedian provides the English voice of the podracing announcer in *The Phantom Menace*. Audiences might recognize him from his work on the improv show, *Whose Line is it Anyway?*

ROSE BYRNE AS DORMÉ

(*Attack of the Clones*)

Her role as decoy for the queen was one of the Australian actresses first Hollywood parts. Byrne later went on to appear in the television legal thriller *Damages* and films such as *X-Men: First Class* (2011), *Get Him to the Greek* (2010), and *Bridesmaids* (2011).

GEORGE LUCAS AS BARON PAPANOIDA

(*Revenge of the Sith*)

The creator of *Star Wars* steps into the universe he built as Baron Papanoida, a blue-skinned attendee at the Coruscant opera in *Revenge of the Sith*. (**Image A**)

CLINT HOWARD AS RALAKILI

(*Solo: A Star Wars Story*)

Having made numerous cameos in his brother Ron's films, Clint Howard also appears as the droid fighting boss in *Solo: A Star Wars Story*. (**Image B**)

JAMES EARL JONES AS THE VOICE OF DARTH VADER

(*A New Hope*, *The Empire Strikes Back*, *Return of the Jedi*)

This star of stage and screen is best known for his roles in *The Great White Hope* (1970), *The Hunt for Red October* (1990), and *Field of Dreams* (1989). He also famously lent his voice to Disney's *The Lion King* (1994) as King Mufasa. At his request, Jones was uncredited for his work on *A New Hope* in 1977, in which he first provided the commanding voice of Darth Vader, a role he continues to this day.

JOHN RATZENBERGER AS MAJOR DERLIN

(*The Empire Strikes Back*)

Before he portrayed Cliff, the trivia-buff mailman in

A

the sitcom *Cheers*, Ratzenberger was one of the more prominent Rebel soldiers on Hoth. (**Image C**)

DANIEL CRAIG AS A FIRST ORDER STORMTROOPER
(*The Force Awakens*)

Best known for his role as James Bond, the English plays the part of a noteworthy trooper in *The Force Awakens*. He was the armored soldier who fell for Rey's mind trick to set her free on Starkiller Base.

SIMON PEGG AS UNKAR PLUTT
(*The Force Awakens*)

The English actor known for his roles in *Shaun of the Dead* (2004) and *Star Trek* (2009) fills the costume and supplies the voice for the Jakku junk trader, Unkar Plutt. Pegg also voiced the bounty hunter Dengar in the animated series, *Star Wars: The Clone Wars*.

THOMAS BRODIE-SANGSTER AS PETTY OFFICER THANISSON
(*The Force Awakens*)

Before he was a member of the First Order, this young English actor could be found in *Game of Thrones* (2011), *Maze Runner* (2014), and as the voice of Ferb in *Phineas and Ferb*.

JUSTIN THEROUX AS THE MASTER CODEBREAKER
(*The Last Jedi*)

Actor and screenwriter Justin Theroux's work includes acting credits in *Zoolander* (2001), *Mulholland Drive* (2001), and as the voice of Tramp in the live-action adaptation of *Lady and the Tramp* (2019). He sports a mustache in his cameo role as the Master Codebreaker in *The Last Jedi*. (**Image D**)

GARETH EDWARDS AS A RESISTANCE SOLDIER
(*The Last Jedi*)

After he directed *Rogue One: A Star Wars Story*, Gareth Edwards makes a cameo appearance in *The Last Jedi* as a soldier on Crait.

JOSEPH GORDON-LEVITT AS THE VOICE OF SLOWEN LO
(*The Last Jedi*)

You might not immediately recognize the voice of this alien due to the accent, but Gordon-Levitt voices the alien who turns in Finn and Rose on Cantonica. Director Rian Johnson also cast the actor in his films *Brick* (2005) and *Looper* (2012).

B

C

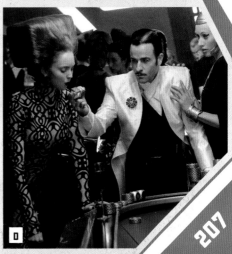

D

94

A

FROM THE CUTTING ROOM FLOOR

DELETED SCENES

THE FILMMAKING PROCESS IS FLUID AND *STAR WARS* IS NO EXCEPTION. OFTEN LATE IN THE PROCESS, SOME SCENES ARE CUT FOR LENGTH WHILE OTHERS ARE CUT FOR CLARITY. IN SOME CASES, THE PLOT ITSELF SHIFTS DURING THE LATER STAGES OF THE FILM'S PRODUCTION. THANKFULLY, THAT LEAVES US WITH DELETED SCENES RELEASED AS BONUS FEATURES AFTER THE FILM'S DEBUT. THESE ARE SOME OF THE BEST SCENES THAT DIDN'T MAKE THE FINAL CUT.

ANAKIN SKYWALKER'S FIGHT WITH GREEDO
(*The Phantom Menace*)

This deleted scene depicts a childhood scuffle between Anakin Skywalker and a young Greedo. In the scene, Greedo receives some advice from his friend Wald: "Starting trouble again, Greedo? EVERYONE knows that YOU shouldn't attack someone FIRST." The line foreshadows the alien's fate confronting Han Solo in *A New Hope*.

PADMÉ AMIDALA'S FAMILY REUNION
(*Attack of the Clones*)

Padmé Amidala introduces Anakin Skywalker to her family back on Naboo in this deleted scene. The situation takes an awkward turn when Padmé's sister assumes Anakin is her boyfriend. The senator corrects her, saying that their relationship is "strictly professional."

YODA'S DAGOBAH ARRIVAL
(*Revenge of the Sith*)

This deleted scene depicts Yoda's arrival on the swamp planet Dagobah, the planet that will serve as his home for the next two decades in exile.

IMPERIAL CADET HAN SOLO
(*Solo: A Star Wars Story*)

In the final cut of the film, we see Han Solo enlist in the Imperial Navy and immediately flash forward to him fighting on the muddy planet of Mimban. His years as an Imperial cadet were cut, but featured his reckless flying as a TIE fighter pilot and trial before an Imperial tribunal.

ROGUE ONE'S BEACH ESCAPE
(*Rogue One: A Star Wars Story*)

Though not part of the final plot, the teaser trailer for *Rogue One: A Star Wars Story* showed Jyn Erso running across the beach on Scarif with the Death Star plans in hand. In the final film, Jyn never left the Citadel facility with the data tapes.

LUKE SKYWALKER AND BIGGS DARKLIGHTER
(*A New Hope*)

The shooting script for *A New Hope* included more backstory on the friendship of Luke Skywalker and his childhood friend, Biggs Darklighter. The deleted scene, intended for the first act of the film, shows Biggs' return to Tatooine while on break from the academy. He shares with Luke his plan to defect to the Rebellion. In the final cut of the film, we don't meet Biggs until Luke's arrival at the rebel base in the film's third act. (**Image A**)

WAMPAS IN ECHO BASE
(*The Empire Strikes Back*)

In a subplot largely cut from the final film, the wampa ice creatures were originally envisioned as a constant menace to the rebels on Hoth. In one cut scene, rebel soldiers battled against the creatures inside the halls of Echo Base.

TATOOINE SANDSTORM
(*Return of the Jedi*)

After their escape from Jabba the Hutt, our heroes head back to their ships to depart Tatooine. In this deleted scene, they face a brutal sandstorm. While it featured a nice character moment of Han Solo thanking Luke Skywalker for the rescue, it was ultimately unnecessary and cut from the film.

SNOWSPEEDER CHASE
(*The Force Awakens*)

Finn and Rey in a stolen First Order snowspeeder, pursued by First Order stormtroopers. The scene ends with Finn making a precision blaster shot to shake the pursuers.

AHCH-TO NIGHT PARTY
(*The Last Jedi*)

Luke Skywalker teaches Rey a valuable lesson in perception by telling her that the nearby caretaker village is under attack. As she races to save the villagers, lightsaber in hand, she arrives to realize it's not an attack at all. It's merely a celebration among the native beings. (**Image B**)

B

95

ON LOCATION

REAL-WORLD LOCATIONS FOR SOME OF THE MOST ICONIC PLACES IN THE GALAXY

THE EXOTIC PLANETS FOUND IN A GALAXY FAR, FAR AWAY ARE SOMETIMES CLOSER THAN YOU MIGHT THINK. MANY OF THE PLACES WE VISIT IN THE FILMS ARE SHOT ON LOCATION SOME OF OUR OWN PLANET'S MOST EXTREME PLACES. THESE ARE SOME OF THE REAL-WORLD LOCATIONS USED TO CREATE THE MOST ICONIC PLACES IN THE GALAXY.

TUNISIA

(*A New Hope*, *Return of the Jedi*, *The Phantom Menace*, *Attack of the Clones*)

This North African country is the perfect location for Tatooine and hosts the first day of filming on *A New Hope* when production begins in 1976. A rare storm strikes during the two-week shooting schedule, adding to the considerable challenges in filming in such a harsh location. History repeats itself twenty years later during when the production of *The Phantom Menace* returns to Tunisia. Yet another rare storm causes considerable damage to the full-size podracers that are flown in from England. (**Image A**)

GUILIN, CHINA
(*Revenge of the Sith*)

Photography from this prefecture in China serve as background slates for the Wookiee home world of Kashyyyk in *Revenge of the Sith*. The area's unique mountainous terrain is the perfect stand-in for the tree-covered world.

LAAMU ATOLL, MALDIVES
(*Rogue One: A Star Wars Story*)

For the planet Scarif, Director Gareth Edwards found paradise in the beaches and crystal blue waters of the Maldives. Stormtroopers and rebels have never battled in such a beautiful location before. (**Image B**)

B

C

WADI RUM, JORDAN
(*Rogue One: A Star Wars Story, The Rise of Skywalker*)

The beautiful desert and sandstone cliffs serve as the real-world location for Jedha in *Rogue One* and Pasaana in *The Rise of Skywalker*. These films follow in the footsteps of other classics to choose this location, including *Lawrence of Arabia*, which filmed there in 1961.

FINSE, NORWAY
(*The Empire Strikes Back*)

The *Star Wars* sequel goes from one extreme to another, this time choosing a snow-covered glacier in Norway for its first day of filming. The Hoth snowstorms in the film are particularly convincing because Director Irvin Kershner shot those scenes during a real blizzard, sending Mark Hamill out into the weather while the crew films from inside the hotel.

REDWOODS NATIONAL PARK, USA
(*Return of the Jedi*)

The towering trees of Endor are no further away than Northern California. Not far from Crescent City, California, the crew of *Return of the Jedi* found the perfect place to stage the battle between Ewoks and Imperials.

SKELLIG MICHAEL, IRELAND
(*The Force Awakens, The Last Jedi*)

Just off the coast of Ireland lies Skellig Michael, a rocky crag that is home to a historic monastery. It's a fitting place for the first Jedi temple and the site of Luke Skywalker's self-exile. Porgs are created, in part, out of necessity due to the large number of birds always circling in the background. (**Image C**)

DUBROVNIK, CROATIA
(*The Last Jedi*)

Street level scenes for Canto Bight are filmed in the roads of Dubrovnik. Oval doorways and windows overlay onto existing buildings to give this historic town some galactic flare.

LAKE COMO, ITALY
(*Attack of the Clones*)

Falling in love is easy in this popular vacation spot known for its luxurious villas. Sitting atop an island in the middle of the lake is Villa del Balbianello, which serves as a Naboo retreat where Anakin Skywalker and Padmé Amidala fall in love. At the end of *Attack of the Clones*, they return here for their secret wedding.

96

IN TRANSLATION

STAR WARS POSTERS FROM AROUND THE WORLD

As *Star Wars* expanded around the world, it went with unique one-sheet posters to promote the film's release. The most distinct come from Russia, a country that had to officially wait until 1990 for the original film's release. It's arguable if artists Yuri Bokser and Alexander Chantsev had seen the film, considering the final content of their posters. The Hungarian poster created to mark its 1980 release is also unique, with its unknown lizard creature and heavily stylized portrayal of Darth Vader.

UNITED STATES, 1977

SPAIN, 1977

POLAND, 1978

JAPAN, 1978

HUNGARY, 1980

RUSSIA, 1990

97

THEMATICALLY SPEAKING

ICONIC MUSICAL THEMES OF *STAR WARS* CHARACTERS/GROUPS

ONE OF THE MOST ENDURING AND ICONIC ELEMENTS OF *STAR WARS* IS ITS ORCHESTRAL SCORE. JOHN WILLIAMS'S POWERFUL THEMES ARE NOT ONLY TIMELESS, SOME HAVE BECOME INSTANTLY RECOGNIZABLE IN POPULAR CULTURE. NOTHING TAKES YOU TO THE *STAR WARS* GALAXY QUITE LIKE THESE MUSICAL THEMES, EACH WRITTEN TO REPRESENT DISTINCTIVE CHARACTERS OR EMOTIONAL MOMENTS.

"MAIN THEME"

It's hard to imagine a world without this instantly recognizable classic, but its success wasn't guaranteed. In an interview during the production of *The Force Awakens*, composer John Williams said, "When we recorded the opening and the closing of the very first *Star Wars* film, I didn't have any idea there would be a second one. None of us had any idea we would ever hear this music again." For Williams, returning to it again forty years later was like "revisiting an old friend." (**Image A**)

"IMPERIAL MARCH"

A favorite among marching bands and Imperials alike, the "Imperial March" is as methodical and powerful as the faction it represents. The theme is so strongly associated with Darth Vader and the Empire, many don't realize that it wasn't part of the score in the original 1977 film. It was composed for 1980's *The Empire Strikes Back*. (**Image B**)

"DUEL OF THE FATES"

After more than a twenty-year gap, the London Symphony Orchestra returned to perform a new *Star Wars* score under John Williams for 1999's *The Phantom Menace*. The powerful piece features a choir singing Sanskrit chants, a fitting theme for the epic duel between Jedi and Sith. The movie was so highly anticipated that this song was released as a single for radio stations, television stations, and even on MTV with its own music video featuring clips from the upcoming film. (**Image C**)

"ACROSS THE STARS"

This sweeping theme from *Attack of the Clones* is the love theme of Anakin Skywalker and Padmé

A

Amidala. Their song to convey their love, the drama of a forbidden romance, and the stakes of a galactic war.

"CANTINA BAND"

Inspired by the swing music of Benny Goodman, the up-tempo song that plays in the Mos Eisley Cantina is both foreign and familiar. It's the perfect piece to welcome the audience into this lively and strange scene.

"REY'S THEME"

Williams conveys his intent best when describing Rey's theme in his own words. "Rey, her theme has a musical grammar that is not heroic in the sense of a hero's theme," says Williams. "It is kind of an adventure theme that maybe promises more, then resolving itself in the most major triumphant resolutions. When we first meet her, she has been alone, she's been without her parents. I felt a lot of empathy for that girl. And I think "Rey's theme" needs to illustrate that."

"BINARY SUNSET"

Melodic and emotional, this theme is also known as "The Force Theme." It takes its name from the scene in 1977's *A New Hope* where Luke Skywalker gazes into the twin sunset of Tatooine, hinting at the adventure that lies before him. The melody repeats in songs throughout the saga when the power of the Force is at play. (**Image D**)

"YODA'S THEME"

John William's theme for Jedi Master Yoda somehow captures seemingly every dimension of the character. At times it is light and playful, while at other times it conveys a sense of calm wisdom. In its crescendos, it embodies the surprising strength and power of one of the galaxy's greatest Jedi warriors.

"PRINCESS LEIA'S THEME"

The opening of Princess Leia's theme begins with a series of instrumental solos, a parallel to the character herself who we first meet standing up to the tyranny of Darth Vader alone. As the theme progresses, it opens up into a powerful performance by the full orchestra, a fitting melody for the bold heroine whose strength and courage endures through some of the most challenging trials in galactic history.

98

CUTTING EDGE CHARACTERS

THE CHARACTERS THAT WERE CREATED USING CGI OR MOTION CAPTURE

STAR WARS HAS ALWAYS BEEN ON THE CUTTING EDGE OF VISUAL EFFECTS. WITH THE RISE OF COMPUTER-GENERATED EFFECTS, THE SAGA WAS AT THE FOREFRONT OF COMPUTER-GENERATED CHARACTERS. JAR JAR BINKS WAS A TECHNOLOGICAL BREAKTHROUGH, REPRESENTING THE FIRST TIME A MAJOR CHARACTER WAS ENTIRELY COMPUTER GENERATED IN A LIVE ACTION PICTURE. THIS BREAKTHROUGH BY INDUSTRIAL LIGHT & MAGIC PAVED THE WAY FOR MORE TO COME.
WHILE SOME CHARACTERS ARE SO FANTASTICAL THEY COULDN'T POSSIBLY BE PULLED OFF IN REAL LIFE, VIEWERS MIGHT NOT REALIZE THAT ALL CLONE TROOPERS SEEN IN ARMOR WERE COMPUTER GENERATED AS WELL. NO PHYSICAL ARMOR SETS WERE USED FOR THE PREQUEL TRILOGY OF FILMS.

A

B

C

D

JAR JAR BINKS
(*The Phantom Menace*, *Attack of the Clones*, *Revenge of the Sith*) (**Image A**)

WATTO
(*The Phantom Menace*, *Attack of the Clones*) (**Image B**)

CAPTAIN TARPALS
(*The Phantom Menace*) (**Image C**)

SEBULBA
(*The Phantom Menace*) (**Image D**)

DEXTER JETTSTER
(*Attack of the Clones*) (**Image E**)

POGGLE THE LESSER
(*Attack of the Clones*) (**Image F**)

KAMINOANS
(*Attack of the Clones*) (**Image G**)

CLONE TROOPERS
(*Attack of the Clones*, *Revenge of the Sith*) (**Image H**)

GENERAL GRIEVOUS
(*Revenge of the Sith*) (**Image I**)

L3-37
(*Solo: A Star Wars Story*) (**Image J**)

K-2SO
(*Rogue One: A Star Wars Story*) (**Image K**)

MAZ KANATA
(*The Force Awakens*, *The Last Jedi*) (**Image L**)

SUPREME LEADER SNOKE
(*The Force Awakens*, *The Last Jedi*) (**Image M**)

217

PUPPETS AND PEOPLE

FAMOUS CHARACTERS AND CREATURES THAT WERE PUPPETS AND COSTUMES

WITH SO MANY OVER THE TOP ALIENS IN *STAR WARS*, IT FALLS TO A TALENTED CREW OF CREATURE DESIGNERS, PUPPETEERS, AND ACTORS TO MAKE THIS GALAXY FEEL REAL. THOUGH COMPUTER-GENERATED VISUAL EFFECTS WERE SOMETIMES USED, THESE VERY ALIEN CHARACTERS WERE MOST OFTEN PRACTICAL PUPPETS OR COSTUMES.

YARAEL POOF
(*The Phantom Menace*)

RUNE HAAKO
(*The Phantom Menace*)

TARFFUL
(*Revenge of the Sith*)

SIX EYES
(*Solo: A Star Wars Story*)

BANTHA
(*A New Hope*)

YODA
(*The Empire Strikes Back, Return of the Jedi, The Last Jedi*)

MAX REBO
(*Return of the Jedi*)

JABBA THE HUTT
(*Return of the Jedi*)

GRUMMGAR
(*The Force Awakens*)

UBBLA MOLLBRO
(*The Last Jedi*)

STURG GANNA
(*The Last Jedi*)

BABU FRICK
(*The Rise of Skywalker*)

"LOOK AT THE SIZE OF THAT THING"

THE LARGEST SETS

CONVEYING THE GALAXY'S SENSE OF EPIC SCALE ISN'T JUST AN EXERCISE FOR VISUAL EFFECTS. IN SOME CASES, THAT SCALE COMES FROM REAL-WORLD LOCATIONS AND GIANT STAGE SETS. THESE ARE SOME OF THE LARGEST SETS AND FILMING SPACES USED IN THE PRODUCTION OF THE FILMS.

STAGE 6, ELSTREE STUDIOS
(*The Empire Strikes Back*)

Known as the *Star Wars* Stage because it was specifically constructed in 1978 for *The Empire Strikes Back*, this shooting stage at (EMI) Elstree Studios was large enough to hold the 80-foot long *Millennium Falcon* and more. Throughout filming, the ship remained more or less stationary while the various sets were built (and later changed) around it. When filming the Echo Base hangar scenes, the space was so large that both the first and second units could film inside of it simultaneously. It later transformed into the Cloud City landing platform, the foggy interior of the space slug, and even flooded to become the Dagobah swamp. For *Return of the Jedi*, this massive filming stage served as the Jabba palace exterior and the Death Star hangar. (**Image A**)

ROYAL PALACE OF CASERTA
(*The Phantom Menace*)

A real-world Italian palace served as the filming location for the Naboo Royal Palace in *The Phantom Menace*. The sweeping stairways, tall windows, and beautifully ordained hallways were the perfect fit for Naboo royalty. Aside from furniture, the space required very little dressing to make it a convincing part of another galaxy.

IMPERIAL SAND DUNES, CALIFORNIA
(*Return of the Jedi*)

Among all the on-location filming sets, this set is particularly noteworthy for its scale. This location in the Southern California desert played host to a multi-story sail barge and a life-size Sarlacc pit in *Return of the Jedi*. The entire set stood upon a raised platform, allowing stunt performers to fall into the Sarlacc pit. (**Image B**)

SNOKE'S THRONE ROOM
(*The Last Jedi*)

Supreme Leader Snoke's throne room is a fitting space for the larger-than-life villain. Red drapes circle this vast space and burn away to reveal the structure behind them. Unlike the Emperor's more utilitarian throne, Snoke's is far more theatrical in nature, having been inspired by *The Wizard of Oz*.

GREENHAM COMMON
(*The Last Jedi*)

For the Resistance base on D'Qar, exterior filming took place at Royal Air Force Greenham Common, a former RAF station in England. The field first opened during World War II and later served as a base for nuclear weapons. Its many bunkers made the perfect location for a secret rebel base.

007 STAGE, PINEWOOD STUDIOS
(*The Last Jedi*, *Solo: A Star Wars Story*)

The 007 Stage at Pinewood Studios is not only the largest filming stage in Europe, it serves as the set for many large spaces in *Star Wars*. In *Solo: A Star Wars Story*, it is impressively converted into the muddy planet of Mimban.

KIJIMI CITY
(*The Rise of Skywalker*)

Constructed on the North Lot exterior at Pinewood Studios, the stone-covered streets of Kijimi City were part of an impressive 360-degree set. This fully-realized space allowed cameras to shoot the action from virtually any angle.

THE LIST OF LISTS

ABOUT THE AUTHOR

Cole Horton is the author or co-author of more than ten *Star Wars* books, including *Star Wars: Absolutely Everything You Need to Know* and *Star Wars Galaxy's Edge: A Traveler's Guide to Batuu*. He has contributed to StarWars.com, Marvel.com, and runDisney. By day, he works on *Star Wars* games including *Star Wars: Galaxy of Heroes*, *Star Wars Battlefront II*, and *Star Wars Jedi: Fallen Order*.

ACKNOWLEDGEMENTS

Creating something for this galaxy is always a team effort and this book was no exception. I'd like to thank Meredith Mennitt and Delia Greve for entrusting me with this mission and the entire team at Quarto for transforming my words into something worth reading. Thanks to Chris Cerasi for his help kicking off this adventure.

Much credit goes to our partners at Lucasfilm, especially those who helped shape and hone the lists. Special thanks to Brett Rector, Beatrice Kilat, Emily Shkoukani, Leland Chee, and Pablo Hidalgo for making this book as comprehensive as possible.

I am eternally grateful to Rachel Barry for being a champion of mine when all of this was just a dream and thank Matt Martin for opening doors for me so many years ago. Thanks to Chris Reiff, Chris Trevas, and Daren Murrer for letting me tag along. More than ever, none of this is possible without the endless love and support from my wife, Jennifer.

TITAN BOOKS

Library of Congress Cataloging-in-Publication Data available.

ISBN: 978-1-7890-9524-1

Star Wars: Book of Lists is published by Titan Books
A division of Titan Publishing Group Ltd., 144 Southwark St.,
London, SE1 0UP
www.titanbooks.com

Published by arrangement with becker&mayer! an Imprint of the Quarto Group
www.QuartoKnows.com

Author: Cole Horton
Design: Scott Richardson
Cover Design: Sue Boylan
Editorial: Meredith Mennitt
Production: Tom Miller

Printed, manufactured, and assembled in Shenzhen, China, 02/20.

MIX
Paper from
responsible sources
FSC® C017606

Design elements © shutterstock.com

10 9 8 7 6 5 4 3 2 1

Did you enjoy this book? We love to hear from our readers.
Please e-mail us at: readerfeedback@titanemail.com
or write to Reader Feedback at the above address.